COGNITIVE BEHAVIORAL THERAPY MADE SIMPLE

Effective Strategies and Simple Techniques to Manage and Overcome Anxiety, Depression, Anger, and Insomnia. Retrain Your Brain to Eliminate Negative Thoughts

Robert Covert

TABLE OF CONTENTS

CHAPTER 1: INTRODUCTION TO COGNITIVE BEHAVIORAL THERAPY

It is important to understand the history of cognitive behavioral therapy to make sure that you are choosing this method properly. The brain is a tricky organ, and there is a lot that is involved with the production and regulation of the hormones that control your thoughts and behavior.

Humans have made a lot of mistakes throughout history regarding mental health, so knowing the background of the treatment you are using is going to help you make sure you are choosing the right pick.

HISTORY

Dr. Aaron T. Beck is a psychiatrist born in 1921. At the time this is being written (2019), he is still with us today. Like many great minds, he didn't find automatic success. He struggled with a few experiments, getting the results he wasn't hoping for at first. After a few trial-and-error attempts, however, he ended up finding a method that has helped millions of people all over the world. This is known as cognitive behavioral therapy.

He developed several studies to help explore depression in patients, with some assumptions created with the hopes the study would validate them. Everyone that starts an experiment goes in hoping to have successful results, and Dr. Beck was like everyone else. Instead of getting what he wanted, he found a new conclusion that would affect what he did next.

What he discovered instead, however, was that many of these depressed patients had automatic thoughts. These include thoughts about the world themselves and the future. The patients had automatic negative thoughts. When we use the word negative throughout the book, it is important to remember that we don't mean "bad." Don't confuse the use of "negative" as a means for you to feel bad about the thoughts you are experiencing.

These patients had negative, dysfunctional, and irrational thoughts that dealt with the world. They saw the negative and ignored the positive. They were expectant of bad outcomes while disregarding what good could come. They saw themselves in a negative light as well and didn't have high hopes for the future. These automatic thoughts were key in helping them overcome their issues.

Development

If you are someone struggling with depression or anxiety, then you have probably heard someone in your life tell you to "stop being sad" or to just "not be anxious." If only it were that simple! If there were a switch in our brains that told us to just stop being anxious, then we would have all turned it by now, right? The reason that we can't just "stop being sad" is that we were taught to feel that way throughout most of our lives.

While studying what he hoped would provide stronger validation for his ideas, Dr. Beck found a new perspective on these automatic thoughts. When they can be identified, they can be turned right back around. Instead of buying into these ideas and basing thoughts and emotions on them, a person can have the ability to twist them for good, improving their overall state of mental health.

It started by helping these patients first identify automatic thoughts. Sometimes, not everyone can see right away that they thought they are having is a depressed or anxious one.

They can come so naturally that sometimes we can't say, "Hey, that's an automatic thought."

Once these thoughts were confronted, Dr. Beck started to give them ways to overcome the thinking patterns. This was when the therapy part would come in. From this method, many patients found not just help, but long-term solutions that they could use on their own, not just with Dr. Beck.

Not only this form of therapy helped Dr. Beck's patients feel better in the long run, but it rapidly spread. Many professionals around the world have adopted CBT, and it is quickly becoming known for its massive benefits that can help a wide array of individuals. Anyone that suffers from depression, anxiety, and other mental illnesses knows that it can feel hopeless when trying to overcome the constant thoughts they are battling with. When we can find ways to break through these, it is freeing and empowering.

Effectiveness

There are many different studies out there that have helped to prove the effectiveness of this treatment. That is just conducted from the '60s when this was first developed as well. Anyone who knows about research studies has to understand the cost and time that goes into them, so all that emphasis on that treatment is pretty enlightening when you look at CBT from a psychoanalytic standpoint.

Not everyone is going to be able to use cognitive behavioral therapy on their own, but many will find that this helps change their life for the better. There are some mental illnesses, such as bipolar disorder or schizophrenia, that need to be treated with medication. However, many forms of depression and anxiety can be overcome with the simple use of your very own brain.

You can go online and see the countless books on the subject. While it might seem like a fad, it is important to understand the popularity exists because it is a method that works. The more you can make yourself aware of the processes and familiarize yourself with various methods, the better you will be in the long run.

The future of cognitive behavioral therapy looks promising as well. The more research that goes into it, the more effective it becomes. When you have so many people emphasizing this form of treatment, it can help to change the world. The more we understand about the benefits of CBT, the better we can prepare ourselves to help different people use this method to improve their lives. We can look at what works and what doesn't and come up with a specific solution to improve our thought processes and overall behavior.

You will have to see for yourself, however, whether or not this is the method for you. It is important to have an open mind when going through recovery. A closed mind is likely what got you to the point of needing a solution in the first place.

CHAPTER 2: HOW IT IS DIFFERENT

The reason cognitive behavioral therapy is so effective is that it is unlike other forms of treatment. It takes your issue and dissects it to the root so that you can resolve the situation, not just find a quick fix. There are ways that you can make yourself feel better in the moment, but when you have continual negative perspectives, it is going to make it challenging to find a solution that sticks and not just something that provides temporary relief.

Cognitive behavioral therapy uses your mind to try to help you change the way that you think. When you can find that sort of resolution and not just one that will make you feel better in the moment, there will be long-term results.

It looks at the root cause without just giving you a quick solution. Think of it like any other sickness. You can take Tylenol, ibuprofen, or another pain medicine to make you feel better, but if you don't treat what's making you sick, then it is only going to make things worse.

You can put a Band-Aid on a cut, but if it is not treated properly, it might still get infected and cause more health issues. CBT aims to help you find a resolve, a solution, and something effective you can use, without any other negative side effects. It is not going to be easy for everyone, but it is something that could potentially help everyone if they put the effort in to change.

Medication

Many different kinds of medication can be useful when overcoming depression, anxiety, and other mental health disorders. Things like Lexapro, Prozac, and Zoloft can help you regulate the hormones in your brain to make you less depressed or anxious. These medications could also worsen your symptoms, however, if they are not taken properly. They can have other negative side effects, and if you have to stop taking them, you might go through withdrawal.

Cognitive behavioral therapy is a good alternative because it won't have those negative side effects. There are going to be some moments that are better than others, but you don't have to worry about "quitting" CBT or worrying that it will end up making your symptoms worse.

There is absolutely nothing wrong with using medications; in fact, they might even help while using cognitive behavioral therapy. Sometimes, you won't be able to do it all on your own, but you can find an aide when you hit the right pairing. You should never be fully dependent on one drug, however, and should aim to include therapy in when possible. While these medications can help, it is still up to you to change the behavior and thoughts that are helping to inflate the mental illness.

Some people will need medications in the beginning, but not everything is going to be as effective long-term. While you might understand what it takes to overcome depression and anxiety, you won't always be able to apply that to your life. If you have struggled with anxiety all your life, using a medication might be helpful to get through in the beginning. However, CBT is different because it will help you all the way through and is something you can carry throughout a lifetime.

Therapy

Cognitive behavioral therapy treatment is going to be more short-term than other therapies. It might still take a few months, but not a few years or more, compared to other types of therapy. Once you learn the tools to redirect thoughts, it is going to be harder to undo this method.

When you get to a mentality of one who has used CBT, then it is something that becomes a part of you. It is a new way of thinking, a new perspective.

There are usually specific goals in mind. You have to look at your life, your behavior, and your cognition and decide what it is that you want to improve on. Your goal should still be a little general, with smaller specific goals in mind.

It is more targeted at the individual experiencing issues rather than a more general sense. Group therapy can be helpful, especially when you can relate to the experiences of other people. Sometimes, however, your issues can get looked over, and you forget the reason you were there in the first place. CBT is going to help you find ways you can apply solutions individually.

It is a preventative method in itself as well. When you use CBT, you will have what it takes to recognize when something is going wrong so you can stop anxiety and panic attacks before they start. When you feel a depressive episode coming on, you can better use methods of CBT so that you don't have to experience it all and instead stop it in its tracks.

PREPARING FOR COGNITIVE BEHAVIORAL THERAPY

There are some things you need to make sure you have before going into cognitive behavioral therapy. They include the right mentality and the right approach. If you are not in a place where you are ready for recovery, then that's OK. You don't always have to be in a tough place ready to fight off your issues. Recognize this, however, so you can work first on getting to that mentality.

Back to the Band-Aid analogy, if you just cover something up, it won't always go away. If you are hoping for a quick solution, know that this is not the place. Also, know that it will not be the way to fully find recovery. You won't have to wait years for results, but you will have to understand that time is going to be a major tool in this process.

You have to be ready for real change. When you are going through a major change, such as improving depression and anxiety, then you are going to have to live a way different than what you did before. This might mean moving locations, starting a different job, picking up a hobby, trying new things, or even just cutting your hair. You can't expect to fix yourself in the same space, or mindset, that got you to a status of being sick in the first place.

There is going to be some trauma confrontation that you have to ensure you are prepared for. If you have experienced serious trauma in your life and suffer from PTSD, we recommend using a professional to prevent further trauma. This book is going to be triggering, with discussions about anxiety, depression, mental health, self-loathing, self-harm, and even suicide. If you are not ready to confront this on your own, that is OK. Only push yourself if you are ready, and never do anything that will end up causing you harm.

Mentality

You have to be in the right mindset before approaching a cognitive form of therapy. Obviously, you don't know how to fix the anxiety or depression, or you wouldn't be here. You can, however, know how to get to a place where you are ready for change. There's a difference between not knowing what to do versus not wanting to do it.

Anxious and depressed individuals are most commonly unhappy, which is enough to make many people want to change. When you have hit rock bottom, there's only one place to go, which is upward. If you have been at your lowest point, you know what it feels like now to desperately seek a place of peace and happiness.

Some individuals are so comfortable with their mental health that changing it or living more positively, can end up being too much to handle. If you only know depression, it is going to feel very uncomfortable if you find that every day you are a little happier. It can be scary to regain hope because then you start to fear what might happen if you lose it again. Make sure that you are ready to move forward and that you are OK with being in a good place, no matter how scary that might sound.

By reading this book, it is clear that you are off on the right track. You have already accepted that there is an issue, no matter how big or small, with the way that you have been thinking. By doing this, you understand that there needs to be a change, and we're going to give you the tools needed to go through with this alteration.

Remember that it is still up to you. We will give you CBT tools needed along with the knowledge of what conditions you might be experiencing, but you are still in control of changing the way that you think.

Approach

Before getting into cognitive behavioral therapy, decide how you are going to approach it all. Start by setting a general goal. This would include something like to better manage anxiety or to improve depressive mood swings.

Next, you'll want to set some smaller and more specific goals, something that you could quantify if you have to.

For example, it could be something like "to overcome social anxiety so I can go to more parties without fear." It could be something smaller too like "to experience fewer depressive symptoms so I can start playing guitar again." When you have a goal, you can better come up with what solution you want.

You might want to do it with a professional if that's something that is in your reach. If you have financial means and live in a place where therapists are available, it can always be to your benefit to seek one out. There is no shame in talking to a medical professional, and though it might seem scary, that is what they are there for.

Don't force yourself if you are going to cause panic, but remember that there is absolutely nothing wrong with talking to a therapist. They have seen it all and will not judge you or make you feel bad about yourself and your issues.

Not everyone has the means to seek professional help, so remember that you can still do it on your own if you don't have finances, insurance, or accessibility to a professional. You might be seeing a professional already as well and still need more help, and that is completely normal as well.

It is also important to consider how you might want to pair this with other forms of mental health treatments. Group therapy might not be the only fix, but it can still help you find other people to relate to and see different issues from other perspectives. You might also want to continue to take something like Xanax, Valium, or Ativan if you are already on that medication and need a consistent aide to relax. Whatever approach to combination therapies and treatments is up to you, but keep that in mind when starting your CBT treatments.

We're going to get into journaling and its effectiveness later in the book, but know now that you should aim to have a journal in which you can layout your goals. This can be a notebook, a leather-bound journal, or even some pieces of paper stapled together. Whatever it looks like, have something handy with clean paper and a writing utensil that you can jot down feelings or thoughts while reading. You might want to pull a direct quote from the book or take notes on the sections that are most valuable to you. Whatever it may be, have something there to aid you in this process.

CHAPTER 3: HOW CBT CAN HELP YOU

At CBT's core are a few crucial assumptions, the first of which is that the thoughts a person has naturally influenced their behaviors and actions. As such, if you can manage to change your thoughts, then you can change your actions at the moment and your habitual behaviors in the long-term. In CBT, nothing occurs in a vacuum and everything is connected. The second core belief of CBT is that sometimes there are going to be things that happen that are completely beyond your control. Rather than obsessing over these things, CBT teaches that it is much more productive to focus on holding onto the things that you can control to ensure you maximize the effectiveness of the effort that you expend in the best way possible. Finally, it is important to remember that feelings, behaviors, and actions influence thoughts as much as thoughts influence behaviors and feelings and assuming this is not the case will only make it hard for real change to occur.

As an example of the core tenants of CBT, consider a pair of students who both did equally poorly on a midterm exam. The first student assumes that they could have done better on the test if they were smarter, which naturally means they are stupid. This, in turn, cause them to feel depressed about their prospects and anxious about the idea of completing more work in the class. Not only has this lead them to avoid taking any personal responsibility for a grade, it ensures they aren't going to alter their study habits moving forward, while also having lingering feelings of depression and anxiety hanging over them.

On the other hand, the second student, who received the same low grade remember, sees their grade and assumes that they underestimated the difficulty of the test, or perhaps thinks they were confused about what was going to be covered on the test in the first place. This assumption, in turn, leads to temporary feelings of disappointment, but will ultimately lead to them feeling more confident in their future test prospects as they have a better idea of what they will be facing and how to study for it effectively.

- Properly interpreting the world around you: One of the main tasks that your brain is constantly working to fulfill is of making sense of the world around you and all the things that you experience. Your brain is constantly taking in a massive stream of data which means there is always something new to interpret which is why CBT focuses on the creation of habits that ensure your brain interprets the data in the most productive way possible. A key part of any new thought relies on making a wide variety of assumptions based on the stimuli you are presented with. For example, if you see a person walking towards you with a gun in a holster on their hip then it is logical to be cautious of that person until they identify their intentions.

While in the above scenario some extra caution is certainly warranted, the waters become much muddier when you factor in assumptions that are made through a filter of either depression, anxiety or excessive fear. When these are factored in you could very easily assume the person walking towards you has a gun on their hip when in reality they are simply carrying their phone in a holster for some reason. The negative thoughts that often form as a result of these misplaced assumptions are collectively known as irrational beliefs.

Due to the fact that your brain is constantly bringing in more information than it can realistically handle, a large majority of the thoughts that pass through your brain as the result of common experiences will happen on an automatic, almost instinctual level. These types of thoughts are collectively referred to as automatic thoughts and if you are dealing with depression, anxiety or phobias then these automatic thoughts are going to be one of the main factors responsible for keeping you in a near-constant state of consternation.

Automatic thoughts are particularly dangerous to those with mental health issues as they occur before you have a chance to determine if they are helpful, much less accurate. As such, your brain has already accepted the flawed thought to be true and has begun acting on it before you are even consciously aware of what's going on. When a thought is both irrational and automatic then you will likely frequently find yourself dealing with negative emotions without really being sure why this is the case.

- Keeping your thoughts and emotions on track: It should come as no surprise that thoughts always lead to emotions, either directly or indirectly. However, if you start from a place of assuming that you were mistaken about the individual, then your thoughts will remain clear and you will be able to accurately determine what is currently taking place.

When dealing with CBT, there are six primary emotions that you should be aware of, each of which can occur with any number of varying degrees of intensity, which will, in turn, lead to a much wider range of feelings overall. These core emotions are anger, fear, surprise, sadness, joy, and love. When you experience any of these emotions, to even a small degree, your body experiences several varying physiological effects. If you are experiencing either anxiety or an onset of panic brought on by a phobia then the effect is likely going to be a flight-or-fight instinct which is accompanied by perspiration, the tension in the muscles and an increased heart rate.

Even though they can lead to serious physical responses, emotions tend to go unnoticed when they are occurring, which makes them much like automatic thoughts in that regard. As such, it is important to keep in mind that while they might occur without you being aware of them, they can still affect your behavior in a very real way.

- Alter your behaviors: After you have interpreted a situation and experienced an emotional reaction, the last thing that occurs is a response to the situation, often through the expression of some type of behavior. While this process is almost constantly taking place, the things that are being processed are typically too mundane to warrant additional action. Unfortunately, if you are dealing with mental health issues then the process is going to be skewed and the behaviors you express are going to be just as likely to hurt as they are to help.

The first student, already in a poor mental state could likely take the missed call as an excuse to consider all the possible worst-case scenarios that could have befallen their friend or their friendship as a whole. This can then lead to additional negative emotions and can even damage an otherwise strong friendship. On the other hand, the second student can simply understand that their friend is likely busy and will call them back later. It doesn't take much analysis to determine which reaction is more beneficial overall.

- Considering your core beliefs: The thoughts that you are going to have as the result of a given situation are going to always be based around your core beliefs. Each person's core beliefs are going to be different as they are based on past experiences and determine how you will interact, by default, with the world around you. Core beliefs can be either positive or negative and will often include things like:

  - *People are inherently deceitful*

  - *People are inherently good*

  - *The world is generally a safe place*

  - *Everything will work out as it should*

  - *There is no justice in the world*

Just because your core beliefs have developed based on your personal experiences, doesn't mean they are going to accurately reflect the way the world works. While this is going to be true to vary degrees for everyone, it is going to be especially true if you are dealing with mental health issues on top of the personal biases that come along with living life as normal. You can think of your core beliefs as a sort of filter that each of your thoughts passes through before they result in actions, emotions, or both.

As an example, if one of your core beliefs is that no one will ever really love you, then even if you spend a pleasant day with a friend, your core beliefs will filter that experience in a negative way and cause you to assume that they are only spending time with you because they feel sorry for you as you must inherently be a burden on those around you.

- Becoming aware of cognitive distortions: Core beliefs that end up doing more harm than good often tend to reinforce themselves through negative thought patterns, which in turn lead to additional negative emotions and eventually more negative thoughts and the cycle repeats itself. These cognitive distortions are especially common in those who are dealing with depression, anxiety or the fear caused by phobias and tend to manifest themselves in one or more harmful ways.

The first of these is by naturally seeing the worst in every situation. If the situation is positive, then those with this cognitive distortion tend to minimize its importance, while if the situation is negative they will waste no time in blowing it completely out of proportion. For example, your boss might have pointed out your good work to a superior during a meeting, but you could be too preoccupied with the fact that you spilled coffee on yourself in an embarrassing fashion during that same meeting to notice.

This is similar to a habit that many people with phobias or anxiety experience which is known as catastrophizing which is essentially assuming the worst is going to occur every time an opportunity for a choice to be made comes to the fore. This is similar to the cognitive distortion of overgeneralization which makes it easy to extrapolate major results from minor issues. This is especially dangerous when combined with the distortion of magical thinking which creates associations between events that are completely disparate. It can also cause additional issues when paired with personalization which distorts events so that it appears as though you are responsible for things that are completely outside of your control.

Mind reading is another common cognitive distortion that makes it easy to assume you understand what other people are thinking, although you have zero evidence that this is the case. Meanwhile, fortune-telling takes the same basic principle and applies it to events instead of other people. Finally, emotional reasoning can make it easy to assume that the way your emotions are making you feel is an accurate reflection of the world at large.

CHAPTER 4: COGNITIVE BEHAVIORAL THERAPY AND DEPRESSION

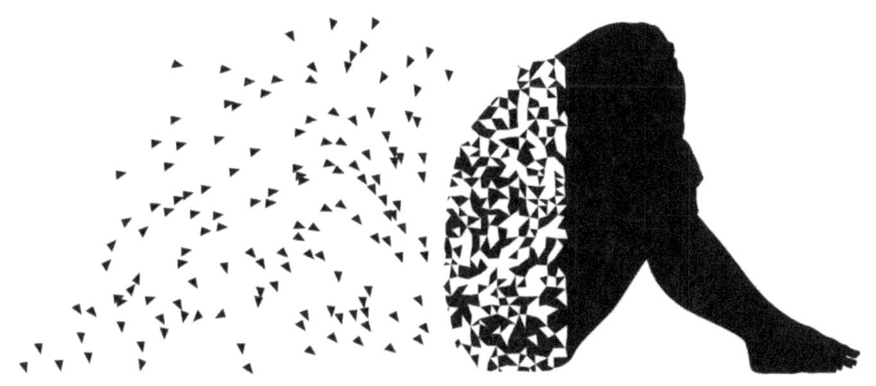

Depression is a psychological problem that a lot of people experience at some point in time in their life. If you do not suffer from depression then you most likely know someone who suffers from depression. Depression is not only costly to your health, but it affects your quality of life as well.

The major characteristics of depression is a saddened mood state when it hits its most severe form. Most people experience hopelessness, despair, and helplessness.

Whenever a person experiences a depressed mood, they often do not want to participate in social activities, and they tend to have problems in relationships.

COGNITIVE CHARACTERISTICS

There are various cognitive features seen in depression that include things such as loss of concentration and memory, you may believe that you are worthless or that things are never going to get better but only worse. You will typically focus on negative things about yourself without paying attention to the positive things about yourself.

BIOLOGICAL CHARACTERISTICS

While experiencing depression you may find that you have trouble falling asleep or waking up, you may not want to eat, and you may lose the desire to participate in sexual activity. It is also possible that you feel tired throughout the day. It is vital to know that depression can also happen when you experience an increase in anxiety. In around

10% of cases, depression is followed by problems with drugs or alcohol.

- 41 -

CHAPTER 5: THE MAIN GOAL OF CBT – REWIRING YOUR BRAIN

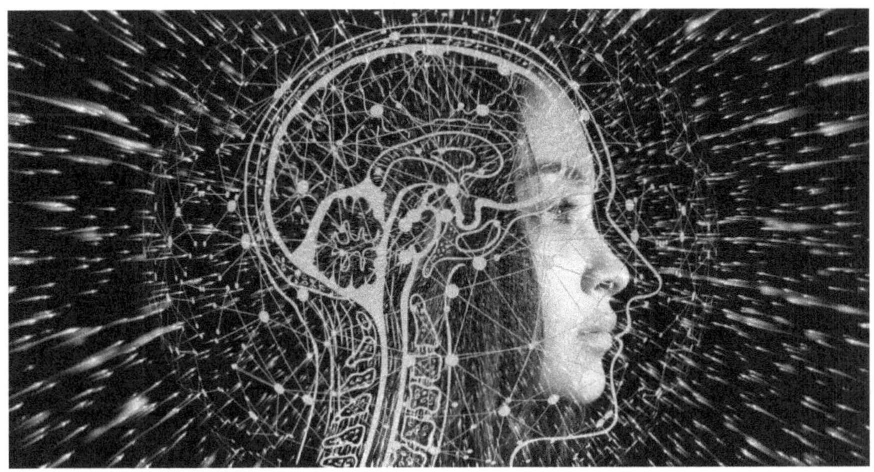

That's right! Rewire your brain. That's what CBT is all about. Recognizing cognitive misconceptions—where they are from, where they manifest, and when they manifest so that you can knock out the parts of your thinking modes that you feel are holding you back. There are several cognitive associations that each person has that hinder them socially, academically or employment-wise.

Benefits of Rewiring Your Brain

Understanding and preparing for your triggers[c1] with CBT can keep you from making poor decisions or speaking rudely to others and help ensure that your temper doesn't cost you friendships, promotions, or loved ones. Anger can be difficult, but CBT is quite commonly used to help root out the cognitive distortions that often lie deep in the problem.

Constant positive reinforcement of negative thoughts eventually leads to a more positive attitude overall. A positive attitude will improve your level of optimism and can help chase off those dark moods that you may be currently experiencing.

Understanding of the self sharpens the resolve. You can try for that promotion or ask for that raise with confidence. You can take it in stride if you are refused without fear of losing control. When focusing on work, you can keep the extraneous, illogical thoughts at bay due to the "net" you have developed through CBT.

It will be difficult at first as you create a CBT framework to filter negative aspects of the subconscious, but eventually, it will become second nature. As a result, you will have a better understanding of yourself and human psychology in general. This understanding will modify the core of your belief system concerning human nature and empower you when you are communicating with those who have not built up a protective framework, all of which can lead to better communication, popularity for your insight, new friends, and work promotions.

Control leads to a better rationale. Often our cognitive distortions lead us to irrational decisions. Perhaps you might interpret someone's brusque manner as an affront rather than a character trait. With someone who looks like an ex-lover or another person that you dislike, it might provoke an initial negative response in your mind. Realizing these things ahead of time and preparing CBT techniques can ensure that you don't fall prey to those subconscious urges to sabotage rational decisions.

Cognitive Behavioral Therapy helps dispel several illusory beliefs that may currently be driving you to make emotional decisions rather than well-considered ones. By training yourself to understand immediately when your judgment may be leaning toward a cognitive distortion, you will be better equipped to handle situations that might have provoked an irrational response before you knew the techniques.

WHAT CAN YOU LEARN?

Do you often feel that something is wrong with you and that others are aware of it on a conscious or subconscious level? Cognitive Behavioral Therapy can help you to dispel that myth and to take your place in the local community with confidence. Once you realize that the world is not judging you the way that you think it is and the portion of your core beliefs that are leading you to that mode of illogical feeling, then the world is your oyster.

Sounds great, but how are these goals accomplished? Well, once you have decided the type of CBT that you feel is the most appropriate for you, then you can begin exercises alone, with a therapist, or even with a loved one. There are many exercises in this book that you can add to your arsenal to give yourself the tools that you will need to achieve your CBT goals.

Be patient. Cognitive Behavioral Therapy is not an overnight process; however, it is known to work very well. The fact that you are reading this book shows that you have heard about CBT, its popularity and efficacy, and you wish to learn what you can on your own.

Why Rewiring is the Main Goal

Understanding your psychology allows you to better understand others. Know yourself and know others. While people come from all different backgrounds, behavioral triggers exist within everyone. Knowing what triggers you can help you understand what triggers others and ensure that you can communicate better with others due to the insight that CBT can provide.

The popularity of CBT as a way to self-regulate cognitive distortions is worldwide. There are message boards, groups, and some other resources that you can utilize or ignore as you like. These resources empower you with support in your own CBT development and reinforcement from others who are going through the same journey.

Anxiety may keep us from interfacing with society. We are worried that someone will "set us off," we worry that we can't have a beer with coworkers because someone might say something that our subconscious has defined as an act of aggression. Many of us have particular triggers that can upset us or provoke irrational behavior, and rather than letting it control us, we can use CBT to control how we deal with those triggers.

CHAPTER 6: WHY IS CBT SO EFFECTIVE AS A TREATMENT?

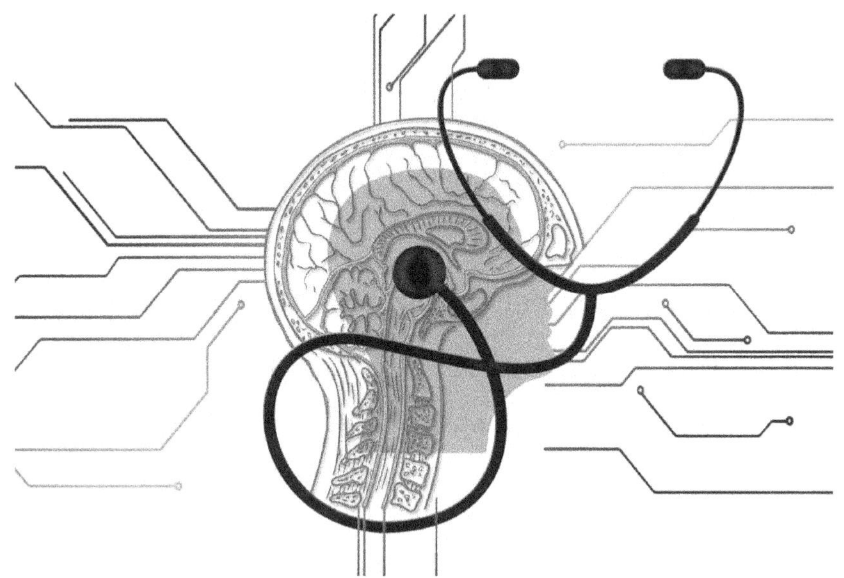

Now that we have talked about rewiring your brain with CBT, let's delve a little into why it is such an effective treatment for many people suffering from such a wide range of ailments across the globe. No pill can be taken or shot that will help cure your anxiety, depression, phobia, or any other mental health ailment that you feel is holding you back. There are plenty of medications and treatments that alleviate the symptoms, but there's no "cure" for these ailments.

Cognitive Behavioral Therapy will, however, help you alleviate a lot of these symptoms. It will improve your life and be a powerful tool in overcoming the thoughts that are plaguing you. So, why is it such an effective treatment? The answer is that there is supportive research in its favor.

1. This study helped show that even in a 75-month follow-up, patients were showing promising signs of improvement after using CBT.

2. This study showed that the use of CBT treatment was just as effective as the management of antidepressant medications.

3. This study used light therapy combined with CBT to prove efficiency.

A common myth about CBT is that there is little empirical evidence to support its efficacy. This belief is simply not true. The more that it is used, the easier it will be to see the long-term effects that this process can have on patients of a diverse group. There are also many different methods of CBT and different approaches that a varying group of people may decide to take. Because of this vast range of treatments, it is much harder to say that it doesn't work altogether. One method might not work for you, but there are other approaches you can take to help you find the most efficient method.

SCIENTIFIC EVIDENCE TO SUPPORT CBT

Data indicates that CBT may be used to treat some ailments. High-functioning people with bipolar disorder and schizophrenia can benefit. It can help with Attention Deficit Hyperactivity Disorder, marital issues, eating disorders, social anxiety, panic attacks, major depression, and more! Many people suffer from one or more of these ailments but shy away from bringing a psychiatrist or psychotherapist into their lives.

These afflictions are extremely personal and have a stigma attached to them that make people hesitate to discuss them. Many rather choose to suffer in silence.

The goal and hope for you is that the techniques listed in this book will be sufficient on their own in giving you the confidence and control to push ahead and no longer suffer in silence.

ADVANTAGES

One advantage is that CBT can be as effective as medication in some cases. While there is no guarantee that this will be the case for everybody, a number of people just like you have used CBT techniques to help them establish better control and confidence without the worry of spending weeks or months (or years) finding a medication with similar results (and who knows how many side effects).

Cognitive Behavioral Therapy covers a wide range of ailments. Will it be useful for you in particular? That's yet to be seen, but if you apply the techniques, you are most likely going to see a difference almost immediately. Most of these techniques can be learned in minutes and applied in many parts of your life, but be patient when learning them. You will need to apply them daily to see results and discover which techniques are the most effective for you.

Cognitive Behavioral Therapy allows you to "rewire" thought patterns. Everyone has trigger events that can make them ill at ease. Tempers may flare, anxiety can occur, and sometimes panic attacks strikeout of the blue. Recognizing what these triggers are, when and where they occur, and in some cases documenting them in a journal to study them can help you understand them and prepare. Once you have prepared and begun to practice the techniques, the process begins to become automatic. Depending on the severity of the trigger, it can take some time, but with patience, you will see an increase in the efficacy until you've created a new automatic response.

Cognitive Behavioral Therapy skills apply to many things in life. Once you have begun studying the why's and where's of how your thinking is affected, you will start to find numerous applications for this information. Cognitive Behavioral Therapy is not just about dealing with anxiety or depression—it can be used as a form of mental discipline to help you in other areas of life. One of the reasons that it is so popular is because it works!

Moreover, CBT is time-efficient. Most of the techniques may be practiced immediately and just about anywhere that you go. As such, you may see results in a much shorter amount of time than you could expect with many other types of psychological treatments.

Empowering

Mental illness can take over your life. When you don't know if you can trust your thoughts or what other people are thinking about you, it can be very lonely. Sometimes you end up isolating yourself because the pain of being alone is much easier to manage than the constant stream of thoughts you have about other people. If you suffer from social anxiety, you know that it will be more challenging to go out and do the normal things that everyone else around you is participating in.

When you suffer from any sort of anxiety or depression, you also know how challenging it can be to have to do simple tasks like getting out of bed for the day, cooking a meal, or going to work or school. These tasks can be exhausting, and on some days, impossible. When you can take back your life and not let mental illness have the front seat anymore, it can be incredibly empowering. You will start to realize that you are in control and that no one else can determine how you feel about certain things.

Sense of Independence

You won't have to be dependent on a therapist or medication long term. These things can certainly help in the beginning, but after a decade or so on the same treatment, it isn't as effective as it might have been in the beginning. For your progress to last longer and help take you further in life, then it is important to find a method that will stick in the long run.

Not only is mental illness sometimes isolating, but it can also cause us to be dependent on others. We might look to people online to give us validation, or perhaps we need the attention of others to feel better about ourselves. We might need constant reassurance from our friends, family, and even lovers that they still appreciate us and want us around. When we don't get this validation, it can be debilitating.

RISKS

You must commit yourself one hundred percent to the process. Cognitive Behavioral Therapy is amazing, but it is going to require a commitment on your part. If you aren't using the techniques or are letting yourself get frustrated quickly, then CBT will not be of much use to you. To that effect, just apply patience and try the techniques until you find the ones that are right for you.

You must evaluate if CBT is right for you—you are doing that right now in reading this book. Keep in mind, CBT cannot replace all forms of treatment, and if you are currently taking medication, we do NOT recommend stopping it without consulting your physician.

- 57 -

Some treatments require confronting fears. Cognitive Behavioral Therapy has some techniques that are designed to reduce or remove particular fears through a gradual interface with the subject of said phobia. You may experience heightened anxiety levels, but as CBT is a gradual process, you can rest assured that this effect will be minimal.

CHAPTER 7: SETTING GOALS AND SELF-ANALYSIS WITH CBT

Setting goals is a valuable tool in CBT that teaches techniques to achieve the goals you set and how to make goals achievable. You can work with a therapist to help you create goals for yourself by identifying your problems and how you handle them and how you'd like to go about changing them. Setting goals and achieving them is a tool to help you increase your power and boost your self-confidence. One exercise is to picture yourself having the power to change the world to be as you would like it to be. What would be different? If you could change anything to be to your liking, what would you start with?

What are your goals?

You can define goals yourself or work with your therapist to come up with a goal or set of goals that you can achieve through therapy. This can be applied to all aspects of your life as well. Some common goals that are worked on in a therapeutic setting for social anxiety include:

- Intimacy

- Creating and Maintaining Friendships and other Personal Relationships

- Asserting Yourself

- Self-Confidence

- Being comfortable performing tasks and actions in public

- Stage Fright

- Being open with friends and colleagues

- Awareness in Thinking and Acting

Many self-help gurus praise the practice of goal setting and focusing on what your goals are for the day, week, month, year, and into the future. Break down your goals into short-term, medium-term, and long-term. Think about what you want and need to accomplish when it comes to your relationships with friends and family, your career or schooling, personal finances, your health and lifestyle, and your development. If you suffer from depression or anxiety, be sure to include goals that you feel you would be able to do if you could manage those issues.

Assessing your Current Situation

Take a realistic assessment of the current state of things relating to your goal. Where are you now, and how far will you need to go to attain your goal? When determining your goals, keep in mind that all of us need Autonomy, Relatedness, and Competence. Autonomy allows us to decide for ourselves the things we do without being controlled by others. Relatedness is the need for satisfying and meaningful connections to others. Competence allows us to put our talents to use and allows us to feel like we're good at what we're doing. Reaching goals will mean more to you when those goals are in line with your basic psychological needs.

It's easy to bite off more than you can chew sometimes, so be careful to create small, deliberate steps for yourself so that you can feel accomplishment along the way. A good example of this would be if a goal was to lose 50 pounds. You may have a big 5-0 at the finish line, but unless you break that goal down into easily digested chunks, your success rate can plummet. Start by looking at the different aspects of your life.

- Career and Education - Ask yourself the following questions: Do you find your work meaningful? Do you enjoy what you do and the people you do it with? Are you struggling with the work/life balance? Are you bored and underutilized? Are you overextended? If you could have any career you wanted, what would it be? If you're currently in school, ask yourself if you're enjoying learning what you're studying. Do you have the time to be involved in other activities you are interested in?

- Relationships - Do you have supportive relationships? Sort your friends and family into separate categories and think about how things are doing with each of those people. Ask yourself if your current relationship is what you want it to be. What things are going well, what could improve? Do you need more time to yourself because certain relationships are becoming taxing? Be honest with yourself in how you need the people in your life. Keep in mind to note what effects your anxiety/depression have potentially had on your relationships as well.

- Faith/Meaning - Most people find meaning and purpose through a connection to something larger than ourselves. Whether you find that connection through a religious community, through the natural world, or simply through our shared human experience. When developing your therapy goals, take the time to consider this for yourself. Note if you are struggling to find a sense of purpose and identity. Ask yourself if you have a clear sense of connection, if you're experiencing enough beauty, what moves you and what your passions are, and if you are connecting to those things that are most important to you.

- Physical Health - Are you getting regular physical activity? Are you finding different forms of movement that you enjoy? Are you dealing with chronic health issues? Ask yourself about the relationship you have with your body. Is it healthy? Is it positive? Do you rely on mood-altering substances such as alcohol or recreational drugs? Have you suffered from addiction? Think about any issues you might have related to the food you eat. Have you dealt with overeating or undereating? Evaluate your sleep schedule. Are you getting enough? Too much?

- Relaxation - Do you make time to relax? Are there certain pastimes or hobbies that you spend time on or want to? Are you wasting your free time on social media and television instead of things you enjoy doing? Make a list of what you would like to do when it comes to recreation. Develop goals around bringing more enjoyment to your life through relaxation and recreation.

Review your answers to the questions above and note how you feel. Perhaps you are overwhelmed and know that you have a lot of work to do, or maybe you've identified areas that you are grateful for and wish to continue. This puts you in the right space to define goals. Don't worry about what others might want for you - these goals are for you and you will be doing work to reach them. If you have an idea of what you want out of each area of your life, the better you will be able to discuss this with your therapist and set realistic goals.

Look out for obstacles. What could potentially stand in the way of achieving your goal? Take the time to proactively consider what problems you may have to work around as you start this journey.

You may have heard of the acronym SMART to set goals that are appropriate and achievable. SMART stands for Specific, Measurable, Achievable, Relevant, and Timely.

S - Be specific. When identifying those smaller steps that you can achieve, describe what you want and how you can get it. "Drink more water" is too general, but "Drink 2 glasses of water by noon daily" can easily be achieved. If you make a list of your goals, you are more likely to stay on top of things.

M - Set Measurable goals and steps. If you're drinking 2 glasses of water by noon, you know exactly what you need to accomplish and the timeline. Your success will be much clearer when you have a measurable goal as you can gauge your efforts and discover if you need to work harder.

A - Is your goal realistic and Achievable? By setting attainable goals you can feel accomplishment and pride. Lofty goals may sound good but when it comes to putting in the work, you'll want to work on something that you can attain. Be careful not to set goals such as never making mistakes or feeling anxious. Those are normal feelings and it sets an unattainable goal for you since it's inevitable that you will experience those emotions and feelings in life.

R - Set Relevant goals. Do your goals align with the issues that you want to address? Be sure to streamline your goals to fit the issues you are dealing with currently.

T - Is now a good time to start working towards these goals? Do you have the physical and mental fortitude to take this on right now? It's okay to admit that you're not quite ready to tackle certain goals - choose something you're comfortable with and that you can handle. Once you act, you will find motivation, not the other way around. It's hard to get things started, but once you have, it's much easier to keep it going.

Examine your goals and revisit them when you feel stuck. Maybe one of the steps was too big and could be broken down further. What can you rework to be more in line with what you're able to dedicate now? Remember to be flexible. Come up with a few backup plans for those days when you can't do certain things because of normal life interruptions.

If you fail to meet a goal, simply examine it again and make revisions. Double-check that the goal wasn't too vague, that it wasn't absolute, that you gave yourself space and time to accomplish it. As you meet goals, cross them off your list.

Self-Analysis for Anxiety and Depressive Disorders

Take the time to perform a thorough self-analysis. Being able to clearly define the issues you want to work on will help you and your therapist find a good starting point and set attainable goals. Depression and Anxiety take many forms and many times we may not even realize we're suffering from a disorder because it doesn't match up to our idea of it. Let's review the various subtypes of Anxiety.

Anxiety Disorder Subtypes

Anxiety can be useful as it protects us from danger and helps us protect others. It helps us to be productive, to survive. However, regular anxiety can evolve into a disorder quickly. When self-analyzing, ask yourself if your anxiety gets in the way of your normal activities. Are you avoiding going to certain places or being involved in certain situations? Is the fear you may feel in line with the potential risk or danger? Is your fear or anxiety around an object or situation extremely upsetting? Do you find that you no longer shrug things off and move on? Have you been dealing with things on your own for weeks or months?

If your anxiety matches up with any of the above identifiers, you may have an anxiety disorder. There are a few main subtypes of anxiety, specific phobias, social anxiety disorder, panic disorder, agoraphobia, and generalized anxiety disorder.

Phobias

If you have excessive anxiety and irrational fear of an object or scenario, many phobias include animals, heights, situations like flying. Many times, there are no direct causes or links to a person and the phobia though some stems from a traumatic event. Specific phobias are categorized by the avoidance of the feared object or situation. If you think you may be suffering from a specific phobia, ask yourself if you identify with any of the following statements:

- I feel intensely uncomfortable when I can't avoid the feared situation or thing.

- I avoid the situation or thing if possible.

- Given the actual danger, my fear is more intense than it makes sense.

- Tremendous fear is caused by certain situations or things.

- This fear has been around for several months at least.

Social Anxiety

Fearing social scenarios mostly because of potential embarrassment. This type of disorder involves a lot of guessing about what others are thinking and assuming that you know the answer. If you identify with the following statements, you could be suffering from a social anxiety disorder:

I fear public humiliation and being rejected by others.

I'm anxious to be in situations such as public speaking, public areas like restaurants and events, for fear of being judged or criticized.

I tend to avoid social situations and interactions whenever I can.

Considering an actual threat, my social fears are excessive.

I'm extremely uncomfortable when I can't avoid certain social situations.

Panic Disorders

Typically having a clear and sudden onset, those with panic disorder suffer from recurring unexpected bouts of fear or panic attacks. Not everyone that has panic attacks has a disorder as it's characterized by those who change their behavior to avoid situations where an attack is likely to happen. You may want to discuss panic disorders with your therapist if you agree to the following:

You've experienced an abrupt occurrence of intense fear more than once.

Those occurrences caused racing heartbeat, nausea, sweating, and/or shaking.

Those sudden attacks caused shortness of breath, light-headedness, chills/hot flashes, and/or feeling separate from your body.

You're worried about what those abrupt bouts of fear are, and if you'll have more of them

You've tried avoiding situations and things that may trigger another occurrence

Agoraphobia

Typically involves the avoidance of places where one believes it would be very bad to panic or have something else embarrassing and out of their control to happen. In extreme cases, the avoidance is so strong that the person becomes homebound, or only being out with a companion they deem as "safe." This disorder typically starts with avoidance of common places such as the grocery store, public transit, concerts, bridges, etc. Some common characteristics of Agoraphobia:

- Avoidance of situations unless you have someone you trust to go with you

- Worry that it will be difficult to escape situations if a panic attack or other crisis presents itself

- You feel intense anxiety when in a crowd, in enclosed places, and/or waiting inline

- You avoid public transportation or fear being in open spaces such as parking lots because of intense anxiety

- These situations have elicited fear for at least several months

- The fear of the situation is greater than the risk

Generalized Anxiety

If your anxiety is persistent and pervasive, you could be suffering from a generalized anxiety disorder or GAD. Common characteristics of the disorder include excessive worrying, insomnia, problems focusing, lethargy, etc. This type of anxiety is spread over many areas and is a persistent dread about what can potentially happen. When one worry is dissuaded, another takes its place immediately.

- Once you start, it's hard to stop worrying.

- It's hard to concentrate or your sleep is disturbed due to worrying.

- You worry about many things most days excessively.

- You've been affected for most of your adult life, but at least six months.

- When worrying, you feel restless, irritable, tense, and/or fatigued.

Remember, we are more than our struggles. We have strengths that can keep us going and get us through new challenges. Take a moment to consider your strengths. What do you think people appreciate best about you? What do you feel that you're good at? Ask someone close to you what they think. Take stock of what you're good at and where you think your life is going.

There are many ways that Cognitive Behavioral Therapy can interrupt and stop the tailspin that both anxiety and depression can cause within us. Taking a close look at what you're telling yourself and reviewing them to confirm they make sense is the first step.

If you notice that you're suffering from whole-body symptoms such as changes in appetite, physical agitation, trouble sleeping, you may be dealing with depression.

Depressive Disorders

We all go through periods where we feel sad or down. What separates normal occurrences of sadness from a depressive disorder is the duration of symptoms including loss of interest in your usual activities, withdrawing from friends and family, relying on alcohol and/or drugs, and trouble concentrating to name a few. You may have feelings of disappointment, irritability, frustration, guilt, and general unhappiness. Depression can manifest itself physically and you may experience changes in your appetite, headaches, lethargy, digestive problems, feeling sick, and changes in your weight.

Keep in mind that just because you have some of these feelings, it doesn't mean that you're depressed. Note the things you identify with and discuss them with a health professional and/or therapist. The good news is depression can be treated with medicine, therapy, and lifestyle changes.

Major Depression - You may have heard the terms "clinically depressed" or "major depressive disorder." This is one of the most common types of depression and on average a typical bout of major depression lasts about four months. Major depression is usually diagnosed when a person has lost interest in essentially all activities and/or they have felt down for at least two weeks. This type of depression can look radically different from different people.

Persistent Depression (Dysthymia) -

Chronic depression is classified by a person feeling depressed most of the time for at least two years. Thoughts there can be cases where this type of depression is milder than major depression, the negative effects of this condition are at least the same. Those suffering from persistent depressive disorder might be described as gloomy, always complaining, not able to have fun, and not able to enjoy themselves even on happy occasions.

Premenstrual Dysphoric Disorder -

Not to be confused with premenstrual syndrome (PMS), PMDD is characterized by major mood swings, anxiety, feelings of being overwhelmed and fatigued, irritability, trouble concentrating, manic and depressive episodes, and disruption in appetite. The dysphoria can be so extreme that many feel as if they cannot control their emotions and sometimes actions which can lead to suicidal thoughts. These symptoms are tied to the cycling of estrogen and progesterone hormones, but the exact relationship is not yet known.

Bipolar Disorder -

You may have heard this called "manic depression" in the past. Bipolar disorder is characterized by episodes of high energy and episodes with depressive periods. This type of depressive disorder can be hard to diagnose since a lot of people will only seek help during the low or depressive periods and not the high or elated moods. Hypomania or mania (depending on the severity of symptoms) can be just as destructive. Manic episodes can make one abnormally energized causing them to lose inhibitions, make impulsive decisions, and when severe they can lead to delusional and paranoid thoughts and visual and/or auditory hallucinations. When the manic episode ceases, the symptoms of major depression take over.

CHAPTER 8: COGNITIVE BEHAVIORAL THERAPY AND MEDICATIONS

If you have an anxiety disorder, a fundamental inquiry that you may pose to yourself is: "How can I improve?" If you happen to bring this up to your primary care physician, they are in all respects liable to recommend you a drug without referencing the best, scientifically approved treatment around: Cognitive Behavioral Therapy or CBT for short. In the course of the last 20 or 30 years or somewhere in the vicinity, researchers have found a few rules that help people conquer their phobias. These standards have to do with how thinking influences or colors enthusiastic reactions and how specific practices contribute either to supportive and versatile passionate responses or excruciating and difficult ones. These standards added to the arrangement of another kind of therapy called Cognitive-Behavioral Therapy.

The Cognitive part (which means thinking) works by teaching people to change hurtful, excessively fearful, and non-sensible edgy thinking into progressively constructive and reasonable perspectives. The fundamental supposition that is: If you change how you think, you will change the way you feel. The Behavioral part works by teaching people to take part in practices that have a quieting impact on decreasing edgy excitement, and by adopting new conduct to confront, instead of maintaining a strategic distance from phobias through a procedure of Therapeutic Exposure to the concern. Intellectual Behavioral approaches for Anxiety Disorders are better than medication in decreasing anxiety and forestalling failure. Still, most Americans have once in a while known about it, and since numerous therapeutic specialists don't have prepared access to this approach, medication is frequently endorsed for anxiety disorders.

Let's investigate the significant classes of drugs used to "treat" anxiety disorders. There are two primary classes of medication most generally recommended to treat anxiety: Tranquilizers (a level or gathering of Benzodiazepine based meds like Xanax, Ativan, and Valium) and antidepressants (like Paxil, Prozac, Wellbutrin, and Zoloft). There are many, a lot more too. The latest research recommends that while Benzodiazepine medications work quicker, there are numerous problems related to their utilization (anxiety bounce and including withdrawal when they are ceased). The ugly truth is that drugs are likewise connected with an assortment of disagreeable symptoms: weight gain, sexual problems (like difficulty in getting an erection and climax), dry mouth, migraines, gastrointestinal trouble, and numerous others.

Another significant problem with all classes of drug treatment for anxiety disorders is that once the drug is stopped, the odds of a relapse are a lot more prominent than after a practical course of Cognitive Behavioral Therapy. The essential truth is that drugs work while you take them! If you learn specific adapting abilities through CBT, they become a piece of you for the remainder of your life, bringing about significantly diminished anxiety even after treatment has finished.

Psychological Behavioral approaches to passionate problems have been indicated over and again by thorough scientific examinations to significantly diminish alarm, anxiety, stress, and fear in an assortment of all-around controlled investigations. It has now been shown that for certain Anxiety Disorders (Agoraphobia and including Panic Disorder), that these approaches have better results and far less relapse than medication (again, when you go off the drug, the manifestations sooner or later for the most part return).

A great many people are uninformed of these discoveries since the medication is by a long shot still the most widely recognized treatment for anxiety problems. Lamentably, per above, medication does not instruct abilities! Mind imaging studies have demonstrated that after people experienced a course of Cognitive Behavioral Therapy, they encountered a lessening in the fear motivation of the brain!

HOW TO TELL IF YOUR THERAPIST USES COGNITIVE BEHAVIORAL THERAPY

Much of the time posed inquiries that I got, like all certified cognitive therapist and supporter of Cognitive Behavioral Therapy (CBT), is how you should say why a therapist uses CBT. To be completely forthright, I likewise discover this qualification to be difficult, since such huge numbers of therapists guarantee that they use this type of therapy in their practice.

I once in a while, meet a therapist who doesn't state they practice CBT. While I am not inferring that therapists lie about what they do, frequently they have been presented to a modest quantity of CBT and are not adequately trained.

Superficially, cognitive behavioral therapy is moderately necessary, as it's permanently changing your thoughts and behavior to feel better inwardly, however, as a general rule, it takes a great deal to be fully trained in how to use this with clients adequately. Although there is no foolproof approach to tell whether your therapist is utilizing CBT with you, there are a few qualities to look for that will make you an educated shopper.

CBT Characteristic #1: Addresses Your Thoughts and Behaviors

A genuine CBT therapist will spend quite a bit of your session investigating the behaviors, thoughts, and feelings that are associated with your fundamental concerns. Frequently they will use what's known as a thought record or, as David Burns, writer of the top-rated self-improvement guide Feeling Good, calls it, an "Everyday Mood Log" to enable you to catch and afterward take a shot at your negative thoughts.

Practically all therapists will examine your feelings, in any event, I trust along these lines, yet what sets CBT therapists apart is their extra attention to your thoughts and behaviors. As opposed to accepting every one of your troubles originates from early youth problems or a horrible past, CBT therapists will look to your ideas to figure out what to do straight away. Regularly your thoughts and behaviors will be programmed or to some degree covered up in nature, and attempting to coax them out and address them gives substantial help and significant life enhancements.

CBT Characteristic #2: Focused and Agenda Driven

Numerous therapists who don't use CBT regularly will offer guidance and be commonly healthy. However, this can prompt a perpetual survey of your emotions and restrict progress. Cognitive-behavioral therapists, albeit intense and outfitted towards your interests too, differ in that they will set an agenda every session to make sure progress is being made or possibly set some structure to make however much progress as could reasonably be expected with every session.

This generally includes a short recap of the week, audit of the homework that was appointed and territories that still should be tended to, time for practicing schemes, and criticism about the therapy. Albeit every single good therapist will be adaptable somewhat depending upon what's going on for you at the time, an excessive amount of adaptability, joined with the absence of an agenda, regularly prompts baffling outcomes.

CBT Characteristic #3: Tracks Your Symptoms

CBT therapists more often than not screen your manifestations or the problems that carried you to guiding, in some composed way. As opposed to merely asking you how you are feeling, they will in general use state-administered tests or scales to look out for the problems that you are searching for assistance with. By utilizing such devices, CBT therapists can spot patterns and rapidly respond by adjusting their therapy to suit your immediate needs. This regular checking likewise permits the therapist and the client both to look at how guiding is proceeding to make choices about how to continue.

CBT Characteristic #4: Gives You Helpful Homework

Homework is a sign of CBT therapists - and any good therapists, as I would like to think. The exploration is evident that if you do homework as a significant aspect of your therapy, you will show signs of improvement quicker and make more progress during your time in advising.

Homework is a prerequisite of cognitive-behavioral therapy since such an extensive amount of the guiding is tied in with learning and rehearsing new abilities. Envision how much more you can do in the week outside of the 50 minutes that you go through with your therapist, and when your accomplished therapist guides that work, the outcomes are even more dominant.

This being stated, not all homework is made equivalent, and an accomplished CBT therapist will most likely clarify why specific homework is advantageous or required.

CBT Characteristic #5: Has Received Certification

This is an association created for merely this reason: to show clinical competence in cognitive therapy for clients looking for treatment. Getting to be certified requires a great deal of preparation in CBT, letters of recommendation from associates, and a broad depiction of how you use CBT in your practice, including a sound tape of an authenticated client session (don't stress, the client must give authorization).

Looking for therapy is an excellent method to improve your sentiments of tension, sorrow, and stress, and realizing who to see makes it all the more straightforward. If you're searching for tried and true and powerful treatment, for example, cognitive behavioral therapy, the rundown above can set you up in the correct way and help you locate a qualified therapist to help you improve your life.

CREATING AND RECITING AFFIRMATIONS

What is an affirmation?

Affirmations are incredibly useful in a wide range of life situations. They can play a special role in cognitive restructuring, as by repeating them to yourself, you eventually begin to internalize them. They can help you ground yourself if emotions or tensions are running high, and you are unsure of how you will react. They can remind you that you are doing the right thing, even when you feel like you are not. Words have power, and the more you repeat them to yourself, the more you strengthen them.

If you have not guessed by now, an affirmation is a short phrase you tell yourself for any of the above reasons. The entire purpose of it is to remind you of something good or positive about yourself or to encourage you to keep going in a difficult situation. They are there to teach that tiny voice in the back of your mind that may have grown distorted over time that you are enough, you are worthy, and you are trying the best you can.

How to create an affirmation

You can make an affirmation for any situation, so long as it follows a basic structure. There are three rules to creating good affirmations that will serve you well: it must be present-tense, it must be focused on you, and it must be positive. With these three rules guiding you, you will be able to design and structure any number of affirmations to help you achieve the goals you are hoping to accomplish.

It must be in the present tense because then, you cannot deny it is true at that moment. You guarantee its validity to yourself at the moment if you are saying it in the present tense. If you say, "I will stop avoiding confrontation," you could argue that that only applies in the future, which gives you an out. Just like you can say, "I will start to exercise," you are not giving any sort of timeline for it, so it is plausible to deny that it is happening in the present tense. Likewise, you cannot change the past, so there is no point in focusing your affirmation on what happened before. By saying, "I am willing to engage in confrontation if necessary," you are saying that about your current self.

It must be focused on you because, in this big world, the only thing you have utter control over is yourself. You cannot control what someone else does to you, but you can control how you will react to it, and using an affirmation can help prompt you to react in a way you feel is beneficial or productive. If you were to focus it on someone else or an external force, you would have no way to guarantee or enforce it is true. You cannot say, "My friends and family will accept me for who I am" because you have no way to guarantee that. Your mind will prey on your insecurities and remind you that you cannot read their thoughts, so they could be lying to you when they say they do accept you. This is a weakness in the affirmation that will allow you to deny it, which defeats the entire purpose of the affirmation. You can, however, tell yourself, "I will take what my friends and family say about me at face value," as that is directed toward yourself.

It must be positive because the entire purpose of what you are doing is restructuring your thoughts away from negative patterns to positive ones. Consider the difference between, "I will not yell today," and "I am making an effort to keep my voice calm and respectful." You go from a negative, which still keeps your mind thinking in negatives, to a positive affirmation that gives you the instructions you need to make the change you desire to see. The difference between the two is that when you think in more positive terms, you are not making your goal avoiding something, but instead a positive action to change the situation to stop the action you no longer wish to engage in.

With these three key features, you are ready to begin the process of creating your affirmations. Remember those three rules as you create your own, and they should be effective for you. This will be an especially useful tool in cognitive restructuring, as you can use it to disrupt thoughts or behaviors that are detrimental to your mental wellbeing.

How to use an affirmation

To use an affirmation, you must first create one. For the affirmation to be the most beneficial for you, you need to identify a problem that you seek to correct with affirmations. Do you have a specific behavior you wish to stop? Is there insecurity that always leaves you feeling vulnerable? Regardless of what the problem is, decide on what it is and write it down for yourself. Look at it and ask yourself what you can do to mitigate it.

For example, if your problem is anger and disproportionate reactions to that anger, write down what you would like to change. Are you a yeller? Or maybe you tend to shut down and refuse to speak to those around you, which you know is damaging to your relationships. Identify the specific behavior, so you can create an affirmation for it. For example, with your anger issue, you might write down,

- *I yell too much when I get angry and it hurts those I love.*

Once you have that example written down, you should think about ways to change that behavior. The obvious one is to say that you will stop yelling, but remember, stopping and avoiding behaviors are negative, and therefore are not appropriate for an effective affirmation. Instead of identifying what you should not do, seek to identify what you could do instead that will have the effect you want. Remember, CBT is active and requires positive actions rather than negative inactions, such as avoidance. Perhaps, after some careful introspection, you decide to write the following:

- *I can try to calm myself down when I feel mad so I do not feel the need to yell.*

This is a good first step: It is focused specifically on yourself and your actions and is half positive. It still needs some final tweaks before you are left with a polished, beautiful, effective affirmation to use to remind yourself to avoid yelling when angry. It is still a conditional statement instead of a present-tense statement and is still quite vague, so that needs to be fixed next:

- *I am keeping my voice calm and controlled when speaking.*

Now, you have a short statement that reminds you to perform an action that in turn, allows you to keep from yelling in your anger. This is a polished affirmation that has a result that lines up with your goal. You remind yourself that you want to speak calmly when you feel angry, which prompts you to do the opposite of yelling. The first time this statement works for you, you will reinforce its usefulness, and the joy of achieving your goal of not yelling will leave you wanting to use it more and more. This positive reinforcement will be your encouragement to continue.

For the best effect, choose a few times a day that you will use to recite your affirmation to yourself at least ten times, even if you may not feel like it is relevant at that moment. The goal is for you to recite it so often that it becomes an automatic thought that influences your behavior. If you internalize that you keep your voice calm, you eventually override that initial gut reaction to yell and always default to keeping your voice calmer. You want it to become an unconscious reaction eventually, so you do not have to decide to avoid yelling consciously. For example, maybe you choose to recite the affirmation ten times as you get into your car to go to work every day, plus as you brush your teeth every night. Eventually, your mind automatically does this without effort as you get into the habit.

Affirmations for Anger

- I am in control of myself and my reactions, and I am calm even in the face of things that make me angry.

- I will speak to others with the respect I expect to receive from others.

- I am strong enough to control my anger and productively use those frustrating feelings.

- I am acknowledging my feelings of anger while maintaining control of my reactions.

Affirmations for Anxiety

- Every breath I take is giving me clarity while exhaling my fears.

- I am choosing to focus on the positives in my life to remind myself that I can live a happy life.

- I can see through the lies my anxiety feeds me and remain calm and secure in myself and my surroundings.

- I am safe at this moment, and I will remain calm.

Affirmations for Depression

- I am worthy of love and care.

- I am in control of my actions and I choose to do at least one productive thing today.

- I am strong enough to get through this, even though it is hard.

- I am actively striving to better myself and my situation.

Affirmations for Stress

- I am prepared to accept when plans change, and I am flexible enough to roll with it.

- I can handle what life is throwing at me right now, even though it is tough.

- I am strong enough to manage this stress and get through everything that is required of me and wise enough to know when I have hit my limits.

- I am allowed to take breaks when I need them.

Do you like this book? it would be important for me if I could leave a short review on amazon. thank you!

IDENTIFYING AND CHALLENGING COGNITIVE DISTORTIONS

Once you have identified them, you can challenge them, which is typically done through affirmation that changes your thoughts, which change your behaviors. Please revisit Strategy 1 for information on identifying core beliefs if you have skipped it, and have your list of core beliefs in front of you for this strategy. Once you have your list of core beliefs, proceed to the next section to see if any of yours follow the patterns of various types of cognitive distortions. There are twelve cognitive distortions that this book will focus on, though some sources prefer to recognize more or less.

Types of Cognitive Distortions

Assigning Blame

Assigning guilt involves thinking in "should" or "must" forms. These thoughts tell you that things must go a certain way, and if they do not, then there is a problem somewhere. However, this can be catastrophic, if you fail to do the things you feel you should be doing, as you suddenly blame yourself for the failure, and use that failure and blame to put yourself further down. For example, you could tell yourself that you have to write 500 words a day for a novel you have always wanted to work on so you can be finished by some arbitrary deadline you made yourself because writers can easily write 500 words in a day. If you fail to write 500 words one day, you blame yourself for failing to both meet your goal and by failing as a writer. Rather than being motivating, you find yourself feeling demotivated because you already failed once so you are doomed to continue to do so.

Catastrophizing

Catastrophizing involves assuming the worst-case scenario will always happen. For example, if your spouse is late for work, instead of assuming traffic is bad, as most reasonable people will do, someone with a tendency to catastrophize instead decides that clearly, his or her spouse got into a devastating car crash and is dead somewhere. This thinking is not rational or realistic, and anyone looking at the situation would recognize the flaw in that reasoning, but to the person with the catastrophizing mindset, they seem completely reasonable.

Dichotomous Thinking

When you engage in dichotomous thinking, you see things entirely in black and white. There is no room for grey areas in this kind of thinking; it is either true, or it is false. This forces you to think in extremes, where you almost always look at the negative sides as affirming your way of thinking. This also sets you up for failure when suddenly, even a 98% score on a test is a failure because you did not get a perfect score. Because things are either black or white, less than perfect is always a failure. These are typically thoughts that begin in "Always," "Every," "Never," or other absolute words. For example, you may have a cognitive distortion of, "I always hurt everyone I love," "Every time I attempt something important, I fail," or, "I am never missed when I don't go to group gatherings."

Emotional Reasoning

Emotional and rational are opposites for a reason: One makes judgments based on emotions while the other looks with logic. Emotional reasoning combines the two, using your emotions to justify your cognitive distortion. For example, you feel anxious about something and use that feeling of anxiety to justify the thought that something bad must come. Or perhaps you have made a mistake and feel incompetent at your job, so you use that feeling of incompetence or embarrassment to confirm to yourself that you are incompetent or worthless. The problem with this, however, is that feelings are irrational sometimes. Something that makes you happy today could make you feel sad tomorrow, and your feelings are constantly in a state of fluctuation. Because of this, justifications and decisions should not be made solely on emotion. Just because you feel stupid after making a mistake does not mean you are stupid, and just because you feel anxious does not mean something bad will happen. Oftentimes, these negative feelings just breed more of themselves, and dwelling on them makes it worse. You feel anxious, so you tell yourself something bad is coming, which only serves to make yourself even more anxious, which is further proof of foreboding, and this cycle continues ad nauseam.

Focusing on the Negative

Focusing on the negative is as straightforward as it sounds: You get so caught up in negative things happening that you completely miss when something good has happened. This is similar to dichotomous thinking, but there is never a positive to it. You always focus solely on the negative. For example, if you get into an argument with your spouse, you may immediately internalize it as a sign that your relationship is doomed to fail. This is most likely not the case; people in relationships argue or disagree sometimes. However, you get so caught up in the moment that you do not see that shortly after the argument, your spouse made your favorite meal for dinner, or complimented you when you walked by. Instead, you dwell on that one fight, seeing it as a guarantee that things are doomed. Of course, this does leave you vulnerable and will put a strain on your relationship. If your spouse were to eventually decide that he or she no longer wanted to put up with your negativity and leaves, you would latch onto every negative thing that happened during your relationship instead of recognizing that that negativity is what drove the relationship to its end.

Fortune Telling

This cognitive distortion involves making predictions of all the bad things that could happen. Because you predict that bad things will happen, you may avoid even attempting something if you are certain you will fail. If you worry that attempting to make dinner will only fail anyway, you decide to save yourself the trouble or embarrassment and decide not to bother instead. The ironic part here, however, is that in refusing to attempt, you automatically confirm that your worst-case scenario happens: By refusing to attempt it, you go from having a chance of success to a 100% chance of failure just by default.

Inability to Disconfirm

In simple terms, the inability to disconfirm is the inability to accept anything you believe as wrong. It is essentially living in denial: you reject every argument or piece of evidence and have some other argument to justify any distorted thoughts. You reject the possibility that your negative thoughts may be cognitive distortions and accept them as true, even when they are not. For example, if you have the belief that you are terrible at your job if your boss ever compliments your work, you will refuse to believe it. You will instead tell yourself that it is a pity compliment, and you know that your work was subpar rather than taking the compliment at face value. No matter how hard other people will try, you will refuse to acknowledge that your own distorted beliefs even might be true.

Labeling

Labeling is unproductive in general as it does nothing but call things names. Name-calling is not a viable solution for problems, nor is it healthy when rooted in negativity. When you have a core belief that uses labeling, it may look like, "I am useless," "I am unworthy," "I am a failure," or any other sort of label you have assigned yourself. By focusing on how you have labeled yourself, you will behave in ways that confirm them. For example, if you are so caught up in your label of being useless that you fail to meet your daily responsibilities, your label has essentially crippled you into being useless in that one instance. These can be more specific as well, such as, "I am a bad writer," or, "I am a horrible spouse or partner or parent or friend."

CHAPTER 9: RISK FACTORS FOR DEPRESSION

Depression does not discriminate against age, race, or gender. It affects pretty much everyone. But then some factors make a person susceptible to developing depression. These are some of the factors that increase the likelihood of becoming depressed.

•Low self-esteem

When we say that a person has low self-esteem, we mean that their self-perception is negative for the most part. They don't think highly of themselves. Such people make good candidates for depression. Low self-esteem not only makes you depressed, but it also takes away all the fun from your life. Most people who struggle with low self-esteem have self-inhibiting tendencies that stop them from realizing their true potential. For instance, one might have a specific talent, but they won't have the courage to take the initiative and see their star shine. They end up becoming another sad case of wasted potential.

•Personality disorder

Many factors are responsible for success. But if we can name the main one, it has to be personality. This is because real success happens in the context involving many other people. But to charm people, you must have a pleasant personality. Everyone is born with a charming personality, but somewhere down the road, we are made to become ashamed of ourselves, and this gives rise to many personality disorders that shun people from us. A personality disorder can very well predispose you to depression. Most people who have personality disorders are acutely aware of it, and there is always an internal conflict going on, which ultimately triggers depression.

•Financial hardship

One of the worst challenges to encounter is around money. Most of our needs want, and most definitely, luxuries require money. What happens when you don't have the money to satisfy your needs, let alone your wants? It can be a very unpleasant experience. Financial hardship not only makes your life hard, but it also predisposes you to depression. Some far many people have taken their lives as a result of not being able to service their loans. Financial misery is one of the worst kinds of pain that someone might face.

·Death of a loved one

Human beings are social animals. We like forming relationships. We feel safe in relationships with the people we love. But then human beings are mortal. So, what happens when the person we loved the most is taken away from us? We feel totally lost. Someone who has lost their loved one is a considerable risk of developing depression. But then you have to remember that death is a natural law, so it cannot be wished away. The only option we have is to toughen ourselves emotionally so that when our loved ones are taken away from us, we won't forever wallow in self-pity, but we will find the courage to move on.

·Childhood trauma

Someone who was abused as a child probably holds the most significant risk of developing depression in adulthood. The thing about childhood trauma is that it is always unresolved. When you are a child, you don't have the mind to take the right action. You are literally at the mercy of your tormentor. But then a child has cognition of what is happening to them. Children have a deep awareness of being hurt. They repress those emotions until they are old enough to admit even to themselves that they were I love you abused. Childhood trauma carries a particularly powerful bomb of feelings and resentment.

•Alcoholism

One thing you have to remember about alcohol is that it is a depressant. This means that when you take a drink, you are predisposing yourself to a mood of being depressed. It is no wonder that most alcoholics suffer from the worst kind of depression. Any sober moment they will be depressed. So, they have to get drunk to forget about their problems. But they can forget about their problems only for so long. So, they have to keep chugging at the alcohol to ensure a permanent state of "bliss" also-known-as insulation from reality.

•Lack of support

No human being is an island unto themselves. Every person needs help from others. If a person has become too disappointed by never receiving help from others, they tend to despair, thus inviting depression. The best example of people who easily despair as a result of lacking support is the jobless masses. They think that the "system" has failed them. This is why they tend to develop a bad attitude against any representative of the system. In as much as it is okay to place your hope in people, it doesn't also hurt to develop your self-sufficiency. You cannot be genuinely self-sufficient, but learning survival skills will do you a world of good when the people you expected to come through fail you.

•Eccentricity

When I talk about eccentric individuals, I really don't mean those people that defy society to make a statement. They are only eccentric because they have an agenda. I'm talking about those people who are eccentric without even realizing it. For such a person, they might feel as if they are not native to planet earth, because there is nothing about human beings that excites them. They do things in a contrary manner, not because they are looking for attention but because it seems right to them. Naturally, society will be against such people, and it can cause them tremendous emotional distress. If you are an eccentric person, you have to develop the courage to stand for what you believe in, and you must not cower to be less intimidating and make people around you comfortable.

•Eating disorder

Food plays a significant role in our lives. This is because food nourishes us. You are not supposed to have too much food, and in the same vein, you're not supposed to have too little food. Some people with eating disorders tend to consume very little food, and this not only inconveniences their physiological processes but also predisposes them to depression. Some people also have a tendency to consume foods that are low in nutrients and shunning nutrient-dense foods. Obviously, they are doing a disservice to themselves. Ensure that you have proper eating habits.

CHAPTER 10: NEGATIVE EFFECTS OF DEPRESSION ON PHYSICAL HEALTH

•Lack of sleep

When you are depressed, your brain thinks that something is wrong, and for that reason, it goes on overdrive, looking for a solution. This alertness can deny your sleep. Most depressed people tend to lie on their beds, and they won't sleep a wink. You can imagine that when this condition is prolonged, all the adverse effects that will come about. Lack of sleep means that one did not rest. And it becomes challenging to take on their traditional roles. Such people find it hard to become productive. And with loss of productivity, they might lose status, and potentially even income.

•Headaches

Some researchers have pointed out that depression is merely the mind's way of communicating an important message. But then this message is not always obvious. So, this might bring about mental unease. In severe cases, one may develop migraines. When you have a headache, you cannot function normally. Headaches tend to make us less critical thinkers, and they take away our capacity to be productive. When you are battling a headache for a long time, it will affect your productivity. Some forms of headaches are life-threatening.

•Chronic pain

When one is depressed, the brain takes it that you are having a tough time of it, and as a result, it sends most of the resources to your muscles. In some instances, it might cause the soreness of muscles. Thus, people who are battling depression tend to struggle with chronic pain. Of course, it becomes hard to be productive and enjoy your life when you are struggling with chronic pain. Also, it is an expensive affair. You not only have to seek help for your depression, but you also have to get rid of chronic pain, which might see you buying various medications.

•Exhaustion

Battling depression is no joke. It uses up a lot of mental resources. Someone battling depression might stay the entire day indoors, and by sunset, they will be exhausted because of thinking too hard. When a person is depressed, he's likely to be overthinking about something, or he may commit his mental resources towards thinking of how to overcome his problem. The brain uses up a lot of resources as it tries to make sense of the depressive state of your mind. It's why you see most depressed people losing weight.

•Stomach problems

Thanks to depression, the brain allocates excessive resources to muscles, to aid the fight or flee response. As a result of allocating mot resources to muscles, other essential parts are starved of energy, which invariably affects the working of some body systems. One of these body systems is the digestive system. With most resources allocated to muscles, it becomes hard for the intestines to digest the food as it would have under normal circumstances. And then, as a result, the victim struggles with gastrointestinal problems like bloating and indigestion.

•Inflammation

When the brain allocates most resources to muscles, obviously, other organs and body systems are left with little energy to drive them. The immune system relies on body cells to fight away infections and protect the body's disease agents. But considering that these body cells have a limited supply of energy, the immune system itself is compromised. As a result, you start to see inflammation, which is a clear sign that the body is being attacked by unwanted disease agents. Inflammation in itself gives a person an unhealthy look and lessens a person's desirability. Certainly, a person with a face chock full of inflammation is not as attractive as a person with a clear face. And let's not lie to ourselves, conventional beauty, which, to no small extent, is aided by clear skin, gets you far.

•Loss of desire for sex

In your happy days, making love is second nature to you. Once you see the person that you are sexually attracted to, blood starts rushing to your "private tools of the trade." Nothing wrong with that. It's great for humans to indulge in sex because, apart from being a source of fun, it is also an act that keeps us away from the prospect of extinction of our race, for sex leads to procreation. But then when you are depressed, you have a fragile desire or no desire at all to have sex. As a result of losing your desire to have sex, you might find yourself turning into a cranky man or woman, which is not a desirable place to be.

•Poor heart health

Considering that depression puts you on edge, and most resources are sent toward the muscles for fighting or fleeing, as the brain assumes there might be a problem, the heart is put under heavy strain to pump blood into the muscles. As a result, there's a rapid heartbeat, which puts the hart of developing heart diseases. The adverse effects of having heart disease are merely tremendous. Heart disease not only stops you from being productive, but it also stops you from enjoying your life because it keeps you from most of the activities you once enjoyed, and should you defy these restrictions, you find yourself at risk of losing your life.

CHAPTER 11: STARTER EXERCISES

CBT is filled with a wide array of exercises that you can use to combat anxiety. These are initially taught and practiced during therapy sessions but are designed so that they can be practiced alone at home or, in many cases, anywhere you find yourself.

The flexibility of these exercises is important because they have a duality. Because many of the help you when you need them (say, during a bout of panic) they can be practiced as part of a daily regime as needed. Ideally, you would do both.

The thing to keep in mind, as always, is that the development of these skills (and the benefits they reap) takes time and practice. If you know going in that you won't do things perfectly the first time, or that you'll instantly feel better on your first attempt, it will be much harder to be discouraged when you have setbacks. And be aware of this: there will be setbacks. That's a simple fact of life. But it's how you react and overcome that determines your eventual success.

This section discusses common, simple discussions as well as two advanced techniques.

- Breathing: CBT teaches us that our thoughts influence our feelings and behaviors, but they also affect our physical well-being. Treating anxiety requires a physical component as well as mental. Think of your last anxiety attack and how you physically felt. What changed? What went awry?

Of the many physical symptoms of anxiety disorders, poor breathing may be the most damaging. How we breathe directly impacts how everything else in our body functions. When we're anxious our breathing may slow to a crawl or jump to a rapid pace. If we're either getting too little or too much oxygen it can worsen the other symptoms, creating a snowball effect.

The good news is that learning to control our breathing is easy and for many is the first step to recovering from anxiety. The simplest exercise is called "four-seven-eight." It works like this: find a place where you can sit comfortably. With your back straight, take a deep breath for four seconds. Hold that breath for seven seconds. Then, slowly breath out for eight seconds. Repeat the process for a minute or two, keeping careful track of the time that your breathing in, holding, and breathing out. Some people find it helpful to close their eyes during four-seven-eight, though it isn't required.

As you do this you should notice everything slowing down, such as your heartbeat, and you'll become more relaxed. You may not see these results at first, however, because it may take longer than a few minutes. Such a short time frame is recommended at first because people sometimes find it difficult or even uncomfortable to hold their breath and/or breathe out for the required periods. But it does get easier with time.

Breathing exercises help to reign in the physical symptoms of anxiety disorders. It's a tool that can be implemented anywhere at any time, making it powerful despite its simplicity. However, one of the biggest problems those new to the exercise have is focusing. It can be difficult to time the breaths when you have worries running through your head and you can't shake them, or if you immediately go back to them once the exercise has stopped. Preventing this requires focus, which leads directly to the next item in our tool belt.

- Keeping a journal: Your thoughts are a continuous stream; there are no waking moments where you aren't thinking about something. It may not also be in the front of your mind but thoughts are always present and always moving. As the adage goes, "I think, therefore I am." It's difficult to recognize everything that passes through our heads as it is.

Throw anxiety into the mix and it becomes impossible to follow everything.

A journal is a great way to track your anxiety. By putting your thoughts on paper you'll give them tangible form. Though similar to a diary, your journal isn't for just a record of your daily happenings. It's closer to an operating table where you'll examine, dissect, and explore your distressing thoughts. This is helpful in several ways:

Better self-expression. How often have you tried to explain your issues to someone only to feel like they didn't fully understand what you were saying? It's difficult to articulate worry or sadness, especially at the moment. But no one will have a better understanding of your thought processes than you do. By laying it out on the page you can practice how you can communicate it to others. In therapy sessions, you can even read your entries to your therapist.

Self-reflection. As we become more aware of ourselves and our thought cycles it can become easy to let thoughts get lost in the blur. If you have a written record of your thoughts it acts likes a map of sorts. You can see what sort of thoughts you had on any given day and see how they changed over time, creating pathways and patterns that you can recognize. This recognition will help you develop plans for going forward.

Progress. It's also beneficial to have the journal of your thoughts because it shows how much progress you make on your journey to recovery. But of equal value to these positives are seeing where you come short. If you're honest in writing all the highs and lows you'll have examples of moments that need improvement. When you reflect on these moments you can better discover and understand your issues and work on better handling them in the future.

- Affirmations: Affirmations or mantras, positive sentences that are repeated throughout the day, are a great place to start. Affirmations are written down while mantras are repeated either aloud or in your head and both make it easier to block out any negative static that your fixed mindset has to contribute in a given situation.

Common mantras and affirmation include thing like:

- I can follow my path to happiness no matter how rocky it may be
- Success is measured in forwarding progress.
- Through hard work, I can attract the love and success I deserve
- I am strong enough to overcome any obstacle
- I can find fulfillment through dedication and perseverance

When you are first starting out with this practice, it is natural to feel foolish, or as though you are wasting your time. While these thoughts are perfectly natural, if you make the mistake of acting on them, then you will be allowing your fixed mindset to assert its dominance and prevent you from making positive changes in your own life. When you are feeling especially dispirited and as though you aren't making any forward progress, it is important to power through these feelings as they are just your fixed mindset fight back. The longer you don't interact with these thoughts, the less likely they are to return.

To ensure you don't bite off more than you can chew all at once, it is recommended that you start with an affirmation or mantra that is fairly close to your current mental comfort zone. Starting with something small will make it easier to rewire your brain in a positive direction when compared to starting with something serious right off the bat.

Once you have chosen a mantra or affirmation that is right for you, you must utilize it to the fullest. This means you will want to ensure that it is the first thing you think in the morning when you wake up, and then once an hour, on the hour, throughout the rest of the day, before making sure it is the last thing you think before you fall asleep at night. When working through it, ensure that you focus on the words, to the exclusion of all else.

- Progressive muscle relaxation: The progressive muscle relaxation technique is useful at the moment when you are experiencing particularly harsh flair ups of anxiety. It involves working to tense and then relax specific muscle groups in a row as a means of distracting yourself from your anxiety for long enough that it short circuits the mental loop that caused it to flare up in the first place. This is large because it is difficult for your body to remain in a tense state that is full of anxiety while specific parts of the body are indicating that they are perfectly relaxed. This means that if you feel as though an anxiety attack is heading your way, a period of forced relaxation may be just what's required to stop it before it gets too serious. This exercise can be especially effective if your anxiety makes it difficult for you to sleep through the night.

While you will eventually be able to use this exercise without a moment's hesitation when you are first getting into the swing of things you may find better success if you find someplace quiet to practice from to start. To begin, all you need to do is to pick a specific part of the body and then shift your entire focus to it. This step is going to remain the same regardless of the muscle groups you are focusing on.

As an example, if you wanted to begin by using your left hand, you would then hold it out in front of you in such a way that it is easy for you to focus on it to the exclusion of all else. Then, while slowly breathing in and out you are going to want to tense all the muscles in your hand as thoroughly as you can, for anywhere between five and 10 seconds. When you tense, it should be hard enough that your hand begins to feel uncomfortable by the time you reach your goal. While doing so, you are also going to want to focus on all of the tension you are feeling in general and focus it through your hand.

After you have finished tensing, you will then want to abruptly change course and relax the muscles you were focusing on (in this case your hand). After you have finished tensing you will want to relax those muscles completely, feeling all of the tightness float out of your muscles, and from your mental state as well. You will want to go completely limp for this exercise to be effective, before then focusing on the difference between the two states.

This comparison is where the real results come into play as it will force your body to realize that it is now in a relaxed state, which means that the anxiety you are feeling can't exist, so it has to abate. You will want to remain in your relaxed state for between 15 and 20 seconds before moving on to the next muscle group if your anxiety has not yet abated.

- Find your triggers: Every person has a trigger, something that will set them off and often results in their emotions taking the reins and causing a lot of issues. They may have been fine doing stuff and then that trigger will push them to be angry, mad, upset or something else. Often those emotions take over the control so much that they will end up doing things that they regret later on. One of the biggest things that you need to do when getting started with CBT is learning how to recognize these triggers so that you can avoid them and keep your emotions under control.

There are going to be times, no matter how hard you work against them when your emotions are going to appear. Someone says something that makes you angry, your stress levels get high, or something else happens. That is normal and as a human, you are going to experience these emotions no matter what other mental issues you may be dealing with.

Remaining in control of your issues is not about feeling emotions, it is more about how you deal with those emotions as soon as they arise. When you feel anger or happiness or sadness, take a moment to recognize that you are feeling those emotions. It is not a bad thing to feel anxious on occasion; the bad part is when you react in a negative way to the anxiety or when it becomes oppressive. Being able to recognize the feelings that you are having and figuring out why they show up will help you to start gaining some of the control that you are looking for.

It is important to be extremely thorough, especially at first, though eventually, you can likely taper off to just covering the ongoing issues that you are still struggling with. This does not mean that you should waste time criticizing what you did or how you failed to live up to a plan, focus on the facts, not opinions.

Once you have gathered a few weeks of data, you can start actively working out ways that you can start improving the common interactions that you have the most trouble with. You should be able to start seeing patterns in your data as well as, hopefully, clear things that you can change to improve the overall outcome for the better.

Once you have managed to make a list of your triggers, the next thing you are going to want to do is everything in your power to ensure you remove them from your general line of sight until you have a replacement behavior ready to go. While you will rarely be able to remove all the power a given trigger has, you should be able to lessen it significantly, with practice. It is important to keep in mind that the early days are likely going to be tough going, but each time you successfully withstand a serious temptation it will get a little easier.

Regardless of your goals, if you aren't already maintaining a schedule where you can eat regularly, then it is important to make doing so a priority. Not only will eating at regular periods help you to feel better, but it will also ensure that your brain has the fuel required to make good decisions. Specifically, studies show that those with low blood sugar are three times more likely to make poor decisions based on a lack of resolve than those whose blood sugar was on point. Don't let something as simple as a lack of food lead to a relapse into the behavior you are trying to avoid. Rather, make it a point of keeping healthy snacks on hand to ensure that you are always able to keep a clear head no matter what.

If you typically have a difficult time avoiding triggers, despite your best efforts, you may instead find it effective to mix up your daily routine to give new habits the time they need to take root. With these changes in place, you will find it is much easier to avoid whatever it is that you are trying to avoid, rather than staring at the hole it left in your schedule day in and day out. When it comes to creating a new, and improved, lifestyle, it is important to not bite off more than you can chew all at once. Instead, you are going to want to focus on adding to one aspect of your life before moving on to the next.

CHAPTER 12: COGNITIVE BEHAVIORAL TECHNIQUES

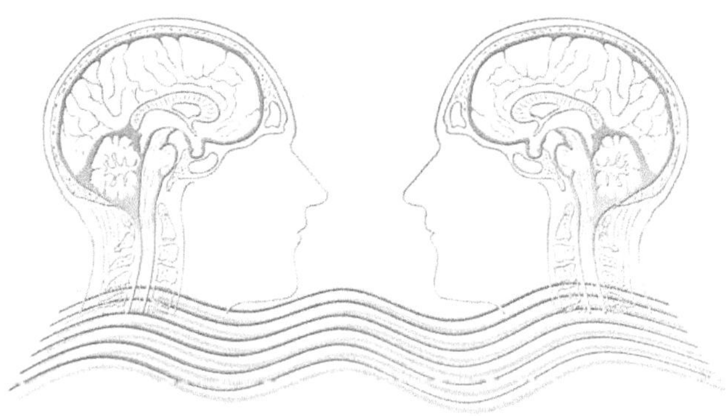

There are countless cognitive behavioral techniques that a therapist can come up with, or you can practice based on the unique conditions and magnitude of the issue. However, you don't always have to wait for a therapist to start CBT. There are innumerable small ways in which you can apply CBT techniques in your everyday life. You can also use a combination of your strategies and those suggested by the therapist to create a more comprehensive treatment plan.

Here are some of the most workable self-help cognitive behavioral techniques that can be incorporated into your daily living.

BEHAVIOR EXPERIMENTS

This is where you establish a goal and test different thoughts that trigger a specific unwanted behavior pattern. For instance, if you are suffering from binge eating, and are practicing CBT to treat overeating, you test different self-talk and thoughts that reduce the tendency to overeat. Does self-criticism following a binge eating session work better than being kind to yourself after overeating? Practice different behavior patterns to gauge what works best to stop you from overeating.

Try varied approaches on different occasions, while monitoring the result of each of your eating patterns. This will offer you objective feedback on the effectiveness of each technique in controlling binge eating. This technique can help counteract or eliminate any misconceptions and offer you the best strategy for combating the condition. In the above example, you may realize that having a kind and motivating pep talk with yourself after a binge eating session can be more effective that self-criticism.

You can also say or write some affirmations that train your subconscious mind to believe in more positive thoughts, therefore directing your body towards more positive actions.

POSITIVE ACTIVITY SCHEDULING

Positive activity or pleasant activity scheduling is especially helpful for those suffering from depression. It works like this (can be worked upon by your therapist in greater detail). Count seven days from the day you begin, and schedule one positive/pleasant activity that you love doing for each day. It should be something that you truly enjoy, and that isn't harmful to you (so yes, no binge drinking sessions and junk food overload).

It could be a hobby you've long since given up or something that you just haven't had the time for of late. Read a novel, go fishing, take a cooking class, paint, have lunch at your favorite café – anything that you haven't done recently and which you truly cherish.

Another version of this technique is to do one thing (each day) that gives you a clear sense of accomplishment. Start with something small that takes less than 15 minutes of your day.

The advanced variation of this CBT strategy is to plan three positive activities each day – one for the morning, another for noon and the third for the evening. Indulging in activities that trigger feel-good emotions in everyday living helps reduce your negative thinking patterns, secretes more feel-good hormones in the brain and makes you less self-focused.

SITUATION EXPOSURE

This is another excellent CBT technique that works well for anxiety and phobias. It consists of putting together a thematic list of things that you would normally escape or want to avoid. Thus, a person suffering from acute social anxiety may find the prospect of asking someone out on a date the scariest.

You make a list of things that you dread and rate them based on how stressed or anxious they make you feel on a scale of 1-10. Work your way from the least scary to the scariest. So, a person in the above example may find it least scary to ask a member of the opposite sex for directions. However, the scariest may be asking them out on a date.

Begin with the least scary situation and practice it multiple times until the anxiety experienced for it is reduced by half of what it was before you began the task. So if asking a member of the opposite sex for directions rated 4/10 on your anxiety meter, work until it is reduced to 2/10.

Gradually work your way through the list with every item, and follow the same pattern.

RECORDING THOUGHTS

Thoughts records are created to evaluate points for and against a particular belief we hold. It is similar to an internal debate where we are challenging our negative/destructive thoughts with evidence to the contrary.

Take, for example, you receive negative feedback from your manager, and start believing that you aren't good for anything. Now, look for evidence that contradicts this negative belief. Think about all the times your manager offered you positive feedback. Doesn't it outnumber the negative feedback? Think about all the instances where your coworkers asked you for guidance.

Would your manager waste time on you by giving you feedback if he/she didn't consider you good enough? Don't they want you to be the best, which is why they are offering scope for improvement? These are the kind of thought patterns that challenge your negative, self-critical thoughts.

Once you consider a more objective assessment of the situation with both for and against your belief, there is a higher chance of coming up with objective or balanced thoughts. The tendency to think in extremes gradually decreases, which leads to lower anxiety or depression over a period of time.

Recording our thoughts is helpful because it acts as a tangible proof of our unfounded thoughts and balanced thoughts. While writing your positive thoughts, your subconscious mind is internalizing them even more, thus leading to more positive behavior and actions.

Thought experiments like these help challenge self-critical beliefs on a rational plane, whereas more behavior-oriented experiments are useful when it comes to challenging a gut feeling or emotional experiences, irrespective of more balanced evidence stating otherwise.

IMAGERY EXPOSURE

Imagery exposure is particularly helpful when a single recent event has triggered strong emotional reactions leading to the condition. For instance, a person has been laid off by an organization where he devoted several years. In imagery exposure, he is asked to go through the entire situation that caused distress in detail and label his emotions objectively.

He'll start by remembering the tone of his manager's voice, the manager's cabin, and the manager's expressions – there is a lot of emphasis on sensory details or imagery. Next, he will label his thoughts objectively. In prolonged sessions, the individual keeps visualizing the pictures in detail until his distress/anxiety level reduces by about half of what it was originally.

COGNITIVE RESTRUCTURING

As soon as one identifies a pattern of distorted perceptions about oneself or the world, it is easier to challenge those skewed ideas. You learn to assess objectively (during CBT sessions) how the belief took birth, why it is incorrect and how it can prevent you from leading a rewarding life. Thus, begins the process of challenging these beliefs.

For instance, you have always held the belief that those who have a successful and high-paying job are respectable folks. One fine day you're laid off from your top-paying job, and you stop believing that you are worthy of respect. Thus, you begin to pity yourself and feel you aren't good enough.

Thus, you begin challenging your long-held beliefs about what makes a person respectable. Being creative, resourceful and thinking out of the box can also make a person respectable, something you have plenty of opportunities to do now. When you challenge unreasonable thoughts that form your core, they can be turned into more objective beliefs and actions.

PLAY IT UNTIL THE END

This CBT is helpful especially in cases of anxiety and phobia, where a person imagines the worst outcome of his fear. Thus, if a person suffers from social anxiety, he may imagine the worst-case scenario of being ridiculed by people publically.

Playing the scenario in his mind allows him to learn that even in the worst possible case, things won't be as bad as he imagines them to be. It is a kind of experiment, which helps a person recognize that even if what he dreads comes true, it will be alright.

DEEP BREATHING

This is another relaxed deep breathing technique that isn't CBT in the truest sense but can be used to supplement CBT techniques in cases of anxiety (Obsessive Compulsive Disorder, intrusive thoughts, etc.).

Focusing attention on your breath and bringing more regularity/control in breathing helps you manage your emotions and actions more effectively. It is said to lead to a more balanced state of mind. There are multiple ways to relax and bring greater regularity to the breathing pattern.

Some ways include guided and uninstructed visual imagery (visualization meditation) through YouTube videos and other audio recordings to calm the breath and let people approach their challenges with a more objective perspective, thus creating more effective thinking and rational behavior.

The best part is it can be used in treating mental conditions such as panic, OCD, phobias, other types of anxiety, and even depression. You don't need a therapist to practice deep, relaxed breathing.

JOURNALING

This technique is closely incorporated into CBT in many cases as a means of uncovering our innermost or underlying emotions. It is a data-gathering exercise for our emotions, thoughts, actions, and moods. It can help identify thought patterns, causal links between thoughts/feelings and actions, and the intensity of our thoughts. It helps us recognize emotional triggers, and our spontaneous response to it, among several other things.

Journaling also acts as a sort of catharsis, especially in cases of depression, where writing our innermost feelings makes us feel slightly relieved. When we describe our feelings in detail, it is easy to change them or deal with them.

CBT TECHNIQUES FOR FIGHTING DEPRESSION

Depending on the gravity of the conditions and several other factors, CBT for depression typically lasts for six weeks. The therapist may work with you closely to counteract negative or depressive thinking patterns. He/she will also guide you to continue practicing the techniques by yourself. Here are some of the most popular CBT techniques that you and your therapist can work on to reduce symptoms of chronic depression.

IDENTIFYING THE ISSUE AND BRAINSTORM

One of the best ways to identify the root cause of your condition is to write down your innermost feelings or to talk freely with your therapist. What triggers a particular behavior pattern? Why do you feel the way you do? Write down everything exactly the way you feel it.

One of the most prevalent and common themes running across most cases of depression is a feeling of complete hopelessness. There's an underlying belief that the situation will never improve. Sit with your therapist and make a list of everything that can be done to challenge the feeling of hopelessness.

For example, a person who is fighting loneliness post-divorce can try to join a local dating club for singles or be a part of a traveling club for singles. They could sign up with online dating sites and meet people who are in a similar situation or have experienced the same heartbreak. These folks can also enjoy a club or society based on their interests like reading, knitting or the cooking club. The idea is to battle loneliness by meeting like-minded people and doing something that makes them happy.

WRITE POSITIVE STATEMENTS

Write positive affirmations or self-statements to challenge negative ones taking shape in your mind. If you and the therapist have successfully identified the issue, use all the positive statements and thoughts to replace negative or depressive feelings. Counteracting or replacing negative thoughts with positive ones is the key here.

Keep repeating the self-statements to yourself. When you write them or speak them in a loop, a tiny niggling negative voice will try to snuff it out. However, gradually, you'll learn to kill the negative thoughts and help your positive ones grow even stronger. The negative voices will slowly lose energy and die a natural death if they aren't fed over a period of time.

Therapists often suggest that the self-statements or positive statements should not be too far off from the original negative thought. This means you don't think you are bad at something, rather, you simply think that though you aren't good at something, you will get better at it with practice. It's like balancing or neutralizing negative thoughts to make them less illogical and irrational.

Similarly, when you are depressed, you don't emphasize on, "I am terribly depressed now" or "I am feeling so delighted now", you simply balance it out with "sometimes you feel better, while other times you feel low, my life too has the highs and lows experienced by everyone else." This makes it a more digestible statement than "Oh! I am so bright, chirpy and happy all the time", which appears more forced and unreal.

The whole idea is that it's fine to say that you are feeling better than you actually are while keeping it well within check to save the mind from disappointment.

You may feel stuck in routine or rut while repeating the same self-statements. It's alright to vary them, create them in other languages, rephrase them or make them more fun. For example, you may want to say, "I am enjoying an incredibly "up" day today" instead of "I am feeling good today or having a lovely day today."

FIND OPPORTUNITIES FOR TRIGGERING POSITIVE THOUGHTS

Identify opportunities that trigger positive thoughts. For instance, you are the kind of person who enters a room and says, "Oh that wall color is so depressing," train your brain to identify three positive elements in the room.

Consciously start looking for positive things wherever you go. Set a positive thought reminder on your phone where you remind yourself to reframe negative thoughts into positive ones.

Another neat tip is to find a positive thought buddy. If someone else is caught in a similar negative thinking pattern situation, buddy up with him/her and work together on the technique. You both can share your positive thoughts/experiences throughout the day with greater enthusiasm and motivation.

VISUALIZE THE BEST OF EACH DAY

End each day by visualizing the best things that happened during the day. You can close your eyes and visualize them as they happened or record them in a journal. Many therapists suggest making a gratitude list, which is writing down everything that you are thankful for in your life. Simply go over the best things that happened during the change and gradually witness how your thought perception changes its negative and depressive frequency.

At the end of each day, make a list of things you are thankful for and try not to repeat the same blessings. Include everything from your vision to the air around you to a roof over your head to just about every blessing you are thankful for. When you start writing everything good about your life, your subconscious mind automatically latches on to those positive feelings and directs your thoughts, feelings, and actions to be more positive.

Writing your blessings or positive feelings at the end of each day creates a brain pathway for more positive feelings, where you wake up with thoughts like, "what a wonderful day it is going to be" over "ugh, just another terrible workday."

LEARN TO EMBRACE DISAPPOINTMENTS

Disappointments and failures are integral to one's existence, and your reaction to them can dramatically affect how you overcome them and move ahead. Our feelings are largely determined by our ability to cope with challenging situations in life. For instance, someone who has just been laid off will think, "What's the point of working hard, developing new skills and taking courses?"

However, a more positive approach during this adversity is to upgrade one's skill, go back to college or take a course that adds to your profile. Being laid off was a business decision directed by market forces that were beyond your control. However, doing positive or constructive things with the time you've earned is totally in your control.

Some disappointing situations or challenges are beyond our realm of control; however, how we react to them is absolutely in our control. Overlook things that are out of your control (external circumstances), and focus on things that are within your control (your reaction).

Chronicle your feelings in a journal if that helps. Write what happened, what you ended up learning from the entire experience, how you can prevent it from happening next time (if it's within your control) and what you are going to do now.

Consciously watch out for negative thoughts and blank them out slowly. This will help you feel even better about things coming up in the future. The acceptance of disappointments technique saves you from playing the victim of circumstance and instead lets you proactively take the onus of your life in a more positive direction.

CHAPTER 13: HOW TO CHANGE YOUR BEHAVIOR

Behavioral therapy focuses on helping you understand how changing your behavior can lead to changes in your feelings. The goal of this behavioral therapy is to increase your engagement with other people so that you can be involved in positive and socially-reinforcing activities.

Common behavioral techniques include:

- *Self-monitoring -* is the first stage of CBT treatment. You are asked to keep a diary or log of all your activities during the day. The therapist examines the list during your next session to see what you have been doing.

- *Scheduling of weekly activities* - you and your therapist will work together to schedule new activities for the following week.

- *Role-playing -* helps you to develop new skills on social interactions based on what you anticipate.

- *Behavior modification -* to reinforce positive behavior, you receive a reward or you can reward yourself after engaging in positive behavior. Rewards will motivate you to change your behavior.

When you change what you do or your behavior, it affects how you think and how you feel.

There are many bad habits you can rectify with the help of CBT. Smoking, drugs, and alcohol may be destroying your life in many ways. It could lead to addictions, some types of cancer and self-harm.

You need to stay determined when you set out to change your behavior because you will experience withdrawal symptoms that may discourage you. Tell your family and friends what you are doing so they can offer words of encouragement.

HOW TO CHANGE YOUR BEHAVIOR

To change your behavior, you need to ask yourself several questions. Start by asking yourself:

- When I was faced with this same situation in the past how did I cope?

- What did I do and what did I not do?

- How did I go through that situation?

- What were my reactions?

- *What were the consequences?*

- How did my actions affect the way I felt?

- What could I have done differently?

- What would someone else have done differently in that same situation?

Think of someone you respect and ask yourself:

- If it was her, what could she have done or not done?

- What would have been the consequences?

You should also ask yourself:

- If I had paused or thought about it first, would I have done the same thing I did?

- How would have things turned out?

Think of the many options that you had and write them down and ask yourself:

- If I had tried these options, what difference would it have made?

- How would I have felt differently?

- How would I have thought differently?

- Would it have been more or less helpful?

- If I did things differently, what would have been the consequences?

Many times we are faced with situations that make us react without considering what the consequences of those actions would be. CBT helps us to think before we act. You need to practice several times, pausing for a moment and taking a deep breath before you act on a situation to help you see the whole thing. Any time you are about to react, stop and take a deep breath. This will give you time to think about your actions and what consequences they may bring and how you can handle the situation differently to achieve better results. By taking a deep breath and pausing, you will have the option to consider which action you will take.

CONSIDER ALL THE OPTIONS

Think about all the options available. How did you handle similar situations in the past? And how they turned out? How would other people in similar circumstances act? And then you take action. Make the right decisions and you will not regret it.

Look at all the options available and ask yourself:

- Is this the right choice?

- What will the consequence be?

COPING WITH MOOD DISORDERS

Many times in your life you will be faced with a crisis. At such distressing times, you may act involuntarily and regret it later. Try the following recommendations to cope with anxiety, depression and other conditions.

- Pause and take a breathe

- Relax

- Change your behavior by doing things differently from the way you normally do.

- Do other activities you enjoy that will divert your attention.

- Play calming music or your favorite music.

- Dance around.

- Do some exercises such as walking, swimming and jogging or go to the gym.

- Do things that are creative like painting, gardening or baking.

- Take your notebook and write down your feelings, thoughts, and anything that comes to your mind.

- Call a family member, friend or chat online.

- Visit a neighbor, family or friend. They will be glad to see you and this will lift your moods and emotions.

- Reach out to others and help them.

- Have prayer or meditation.

GETTING RID OF ADDICTION

You may have addictions that are hard to overcome

- Bulimia

- Alcohol and drug abuse

- Smoking

Alcohol abuse may affect your relationships, your quality of life and loss of control. It can lead to health problems such as alcohol poisoning, cirrhosis of the liver, and loss of close relationships. It can also lead to destructive behaviors such as drinking and driving, violence and self-harm. Long-term alcohol abuse may lead to heart disease, stroke, liver cancer, and bowel cancer. On top of these, you may lose personal property like wallets, mobile phones, keys, and other property. Alcohol abuse has been a contributory factor to domestic violence, divorce, unemployment, anxiety, stress, and depression.

You can change this behavior by making the right choices.

CHAPTER 14: CHANGING YOUR PERSPECTIVE

Many thoughts that come across our minds are based on opinions instead of facts. There is a story about an elephant. Five blind people were sent to observe an elephant. One person touched the ears and reported back and said that the elephant was like a fan. Another one touched the legs and reported that it was like a building pole. The third one touched the side of the elephant and concluded that it was like a wall. The other one touched the trunk and said that it was like a snake while the fifth one touched the tusk and reported that it was hard and firm. You can see how people differ about the same thing.

LOOKING AT DIFFERENT PERSPECTIVES

There are many different perspectives on one thing. That is why in a court of justice, the judge or jury calls many witnesses, lawyers/advocates and prosecutors to give evidence. Each one of them gives evidence based on what they saw, heard and felt about the event or situation.

We may look at something and make our judgments about it without looking from different perspectives. At first, it may seem one way, but if we take time to explore other possibilities we may end up with different facts and opinions about the whole thing.

We attach different meanings to situations, events, interactions, conversations and all that is happening to us, around us, to others and the world. Instead of seeing things the way they are, we make our interpretations about them.

Do you need to be realistic about what you are going through? Do you need to drink alcohol? Do you have to smoke? Why are you overeating? What purpose will it serve? How will this affect you? What are the consequences?

You should be rational and ask yourself what would someone else (you respect) do if faced with the same situation?

LEARN TO VIEW THINGS DIFFERENTLY

You should view things at wider perspectives, what is known as "seeing the bigger picture." Stand back and see the "bigger picture." You may be entangled in negative emotions which make you irrational.

Try to balance your moods with your rational thoughts. Apply your reasonable mind (based on facts) to what you are going through. This way you will be able to respond to what is going on most helpfully and effectively.

Someone might attack you with words. What will you do? The first reaction is to do the same to him. But does it help? We say that two wrongs don't make a right. You feel your moods overwhelm you by doing the wrong thing.

Swallow your pride and think about it first. You may feel like you are choking with anger but doing the right thing will ultimately lift your spirits. You will feel happier for making the right decision.

We all have different belief systems and how you might see a situation may be different from the way I see it. Think about how other people might see the situation differently. Since you may be overwhelmed by emotions, it is good for you to consider other people's perspectives (those who are not affected by these emotions).

THINGS TO CONSIDER

Ask yourself:

- Am I dealing with facts or opinions?

- How am I reacting to this situation?

- How am I interpreting the situation? What meaning am I giving it?

- How can I look at it differently?

- How would others who are not emotionally affected see it? What meaning would they give? How would they react?

- What is the best thing to do?

- Are the thoughts I have helpful or unhelpful?

- What is the bigger picture?

- What is the best way of looking at it?

- If I was an outsider, how would I look at it?

When you look at the situation in another perspective your moods will improve and this will lead to more healthy behavior. Your interactions and relationships will improve. Your self-esteem will improve and you will be more confident and realistically see things.

You will look at people and situations differently. You will be able to communicate more effectively and treat others with empathy. You will feel better about yourself and be happier.

The best thing about CBT is you can adjust your mind and your behavior so that your moods and emotions can change for the better. To influence the way we react, we need to change our minds to positive, rational and realistic thoughts.

CHAPTER 15: PRINCIPLES OF AUTOMATIC AND INTRUSIVE THOUGHTS

We, as humans, have between 70,000 to 100,000 thoughts every day that allow us to interpret the world, describe what is occurring and allow us to make sense of our surroundings. We interpret and give things their meanings without even realizing it. We can decide if things are nasty or pleasant, bad or good, safe or dangerous, etc.

THE SCIENCE OF AUTOMATIC THOUGHTS

Thoughts are electro-chemical impulses that take place in our minds, which means that they are not statements of fact. Cognitive-behavioral therapy has shown that it is not events that cause our emotions and reactions, but the meaning that our brains give to these said events and what we think about what is happening itself.

We all can have very different interpretations of the same event, thanks to what we have previously experienced, how we were raised, and our beliefs and values. The meanings we give to events result in how we physically and emotionally feel. When something happens, we naturally notice things, which trigger thoughts that lead to emotions and actions. Here are a few examples:

- The thought: *"I think something bad is going to happen and I will be unable to cope."* This then leads to feelings of anxiety and avoiding/escaping these situations.

- The thought: *"I'm not being treated fairly."* This leads to angry feelings that make us respond by shouting, hitting, etc.

- The thought: *"The world is a dark place."* Similar gloomy thoughts can lead to depression, which can make us isolate ourselves and do less with our lives.

Characteristics of Automatic Thoughts:

- It can be a memory, an image, words, physical sensation, imagined sound or based on our intuition.

- Are very believable; we automatically and naturally believe our thoughts.

- They just occur, coming into our minds without us even realizing it.

- They are ours, which means they are catered to our lives and our experiences, knowledge, cultures, values, etc.

- They are persistent and become habitual, meaning they repeat themselves over and over. The more this happens, the more believable they become.

THE SCIENCE OF INTRUSIVE THOUGHTS

Intrusive thoughts are unwanted thoughts that are stuck in our minds and can cause us distress. They pop up from nowhere and cause us a great deal of anxiety. Intrusive thoughts are often focused on violent, sexual, or socially unacceptable images. Many people fear they commit the acts they picture in their minds, which can lead to feelings of obsession and compulsive actions.

The difference between intrusive and automatic thoughts is that intrusive ones are naturally distressing, which can cause negative actions to result from them. Intrusive thoughts are typically about negative things because they are important to us and we tend to pay loads of attention to them.

Intrusive thoughts naturally latch onto things that are priorities to you in life. If you love animals, for instance, you may have a thought that pops into your head of you harming an animal, which can shake your values up tremendously.

Yes, intrusive thoughts are normal! What sets everyday people apart from those that struggle with these thoughts is what they decide to do with them. It is when you fail to ignore them and dig deeper that you add 'meat' to these negative thought processes and create a narrative from them in your mind.

<u>Examples of intrusive thoughts:</u>

- Touching someone inappropriately

- The desire to kiss another person

- To hurt someone you care about

- To confess to things you have not done

HOW TO CONFRONT AND CONQUER AUTOMATIC AND INTRUSIVE THOUGHTS

So, how does one go about managing their automatic thoughts and intrusive urges? It is very simple; the problem only arises when you pay far too much attention to the urge that comes to mind. If you are very religious, for instance, and you have the urge to shout something obscene during service, ignore this thought.

The more you focus on what pops into your mind, the stronger the urge will become. In other words, the more you give it your attention, the more power you are fueling it with to take control of you.

Learn to label these thoughts as intrusive and remind yourself that they happen automatically. They are not ultimately up to you. When you accept and allow them to happen while not giving them the time of day, you can allow time to pass more positively. Do not engage with the thoughts or actively push them out of your mind, for this is when people become obsessed with them.

Instead, figure out what these thoughts mean to you. Remember, less is more and to give yourself time. Continue with whatever you are doing when these automatic and intrusive thoughts disrupt you.

UNDERSTANDING THE 'THINKING-FEELING-ACTING' CONNECTION

Let's relax for a moment, shall we? I want you to clear your mind and imagine the following situation:

You are walking down the street and you see someone you know on the opposite side of the street. You smile big and wave, yet they don't acknowledge you and keep walking. How do you feel?

Well, the way you feel about this situation is going to depend on your thoughts. If you think –

- "What is the matter? Have I done something to upset them?"

- Thinking like this will likely cause you to feel worried or anxious.

- "Why did they not respond? They must no longer like me..."

- Thinking like this will likely cause you to feel saddened.

- "What is their problem? What is wrong with them?"

- Thinking like this will likely cause you to feel anger.

- "Oh, I guess they did not notice me."

- Thinking like this will likely cause you to feel mildly disappointed.

THE ABC MODEL

The point is, the situations you face every day do not dictate how you ultimately feel, the way that you feel solely depends on the thoughts you have in response to the situation. This relationship is commonly referred to as the ABC model.

1. First, at A, we have a situation or *Activating Event.* (A)

2. The result is feeling or *Consequence.* (C)

3. However, what many of us are unaware of is the thought or *Belief* that links A and C together. (B)

a. These thoughts are commonly referred to as automatic thoughts since they arise immediately and automatically. These types of thoughts help to determine the way we feel and just how strongly we feel it.

Let's take a gander back at our example from above again. We started at A with the activating event that led to B, which were the thoughts we had, that led us to C, how we ended up feeling thanks to those thoughts. The automatic thoughts we have can greatly depend on the mood and the way we are feeling at that time. For instance, if you are already feeling anxious, you are more likely to feel anxious when a situation like that of the above arises. Our thoughts and moods are often congruent. Because thoughts and feelings are so strongly connected, it is of great importance to become aware of how outside influences make us feel.

If you are anxious, you will naturally have anxious thoughts. If you are sad, you will become depressed. All these feelings can turn into a vicious cycle that can leave a negative mark on your life and fulfillment. If you can notice your thoughts and how they affect your mood, you can have better power on how they affect your future thoughts and actions and eliminate them before they become too out of hand.

THINKING-FEELING-ACTING CONNECTION

After connecting our thoughts to how we feel, we can now connect the relationship to this connection to the way we behave and our bodily sensations, since all these elements greatly influence one another.

We start with the situation, which can be either:

- External
  - Things we do
  - Things that happen
- Internal
  - Thought

- o Feeling

- o Bodily sensation

The situation then generates:

- Thoughts

  - o Beliefs

  - o Images

  - o Self-talk

- Feelings

  - o What you are internally feeling

  - o Your mood

  - o Your emotions

- Actions

    o What you are doing

    o How you behave

- Bodily sensations

    o Pain

    o Physiological responses

    o Sensations

Let's look at another example:

You are out with a group of people you do not know very well. You are a bit shy and feeling uncomfortable.

- *Thought – "I wish I had something interesting to talk about."*

- *Feeling* – Anxious

- *Action* – You try to say something, but since you are anxious, you stumble your words a bit.

- *Body* – You then feel a bit embarrassed, which results in a tight feeling in your chest.

- *Thought* - Then, you think: *"What is wrong with me? I don't even know how to talk to people."*

- *Feeling* – Then you feel sad

- *Body* – You have a feeling of despair in the pit of your stomach

- *Thought* – *"There is no point in even trying anymore."*

- *Action* – You excuse yourself and head home.

When you are home, you begin feeling depressed. You can visibly see that in this type of situation, how your thought processes, feelings, actions, and bodily sensations all play a hand in how you behave.

CHAPTER 16: GETTING BACK CONTROL OF YOUR LIFE

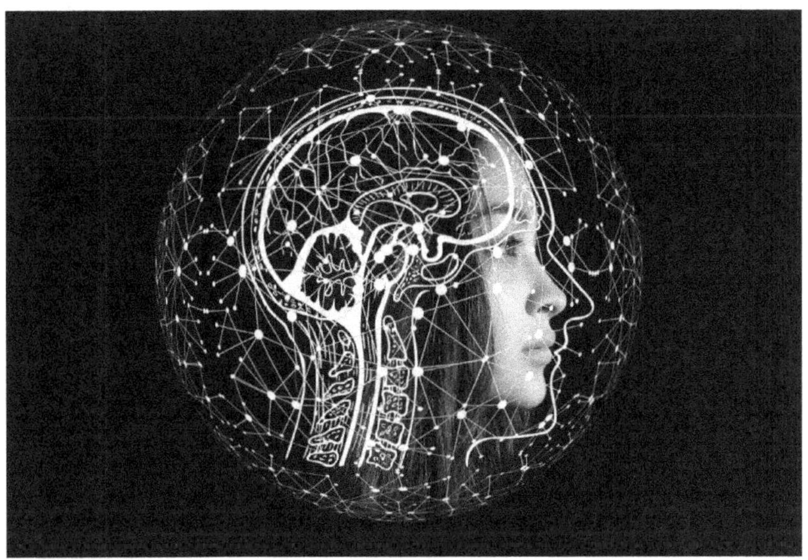

THE IMPORTANCE OF DEVELOPING GOALS

"Begin with the end in mind." – Stephen Covey

Goals play a key role in helping us to move forward in our lives. They are essentially the oxygen that our dreams and aspirations breathe. They are the beginning steps on the adventure we take as well as our last in the path of achieving success. It's vital to truly realize the significance that setting goals have on all our lives.

GOAL SETTING IS CRUCIAL BECAUSE...

Any planning that you do to prepare and set yourself up for success in the future is a goal. From planning our chores to developing a retirement plan and everything in-between, the small tasks we do every day are helping to set ourselves up for a brighter tomorrow.

PROVIDES US WITH FOCUS

Do you think you could shoot an arrow without a target to hit? If there were nowhere to aim, then you would just be aiming at a random object to strike. Why would you choose to aim at random and what would the purpose behind it be? Exactly.

The bow and arrow example is a literal analogy to how life would be without the existence of goals. Even if you have the potential and drive, without focus, your talent and abilities are useless. Sunlight cannot burn through a magnifying glass without focus, and the same goes for you. You will be unable to ever achieve anything unless you focus on your efforts.

At the end of the day, your goals are what provide you with a direction in your life. When you set goals, you are giving yourself a target to aim at. When you have a clear sense of direction, this allows your mind to hone in on your target. Instead of wasting time and energy aimlessly shooting, this gives you something to aim for and hit, a.k.a. reaching your goal.

PROVIDES A WAY TO MEASURE PROGRESS

When you set goals, you are then paired with a system to measure your overall progress since you are equipped with a benchmark to compare it to.

For instance, say you have a goal to write a novel that is 300 pages in length. You start to write each day and strive to work hard in doing so. Then, you lose track of how many pages you have written and how many more you must write to reach your quota. Instead of freaking out, you can simply count the pages you have done, determine the progress, and figure out how much you still need to write.

KEEPS US FROM BECOMING DISTRACTED

When you set goals, you are also providing yourself with mental boundaries. When there is an endpoint in mind, you are better at avoiding distractions and remaining focused on the result. This occurs automatically. No matter who or what meets you along the path you are treading to get to your goal, it always stays locked in and insight. This is why successful individuals thrive on setting goals so they can stay automatically locked in and give their goals 100%.

HELP DEFEAT PROCRASTINATION

Setting goals creates a kind of personal accountability. Goals have a way of sticking in your mind and if they go uncompleted, they do not just go away. You have probably had that "Shoot, I was supposed to do _____ today!" moment several times in your life. This is your brain's way of reminding you to get back on track. They also help you to overcome laziness.

GIVE YOUR MOTIVATION

Goals are the root of inspiration and motivation. They are the building blocks to the foundation for your drive to complete things in life. When you make a goal, you create an endpoint to aim for and get excited about. It provides you with the sole thought of accomplishing it, which develops the motivation you need to keep up the momentum to get it done.

Goals are tools that give you the energy to focus in a positive direction and are easily molded to fit your priorities when they change. They can connect you directly with your innermost desires, which help to motivate you and provide you with something to achieve.

GIVES YOU THE REINS OF YOUR LIFE

The majority of society in today's world is sleepwalking their way through life. Even if they are working hard, they do not ever feel a sense of achievement, which is derived from the fact that they fail to set a sense of direction for themselves.

When you fail to set goals, you are spending your life running up and down endlessly without achieving anything. You are merely just fulfilling the goals of others, not yourself.

Setting goals that are centered on your desires help you to break out of the autopilot many of us are in and genuinely start living consciously. Don't let others inform you of what to do. This is your life that you should be taking charge of in a proactive way. Goals help you to think for yourself and then go out and get what you want.

GIVES US ULTIMATE RESULTS

All of the most successful people in the world set clear and concise goals, from athletes to business professionals to performers and everyone in-between. When you can set goals, then you have the vision to work forward. You are then ensured that pushing yourself will lead you to achieve better results, rather than you just lying around waiting for things to happen.

When actions can be measured, there is major room for continued improvement. If you fail to specify your targets, you will find that things will never really get better, because there is nothing to work towards, even if you are working your butt off.

When you are setting goals, thinking ahead is the key to create an actionable plan. Even when things do not go according to that plan (and they will trust me), you then have a system to review and adjust your way to achieve those goals, since you are steering toward the vision you have for your life.

Everything we do is created twice: once in the mind, then in the physical world. The mental creation occurs when you set goals and it happens in the real world when you put in the hard work and sweat to bring that goal to life. Without the creation of goals in your mind, the physical representation is unlikely to happen.

MAKES US HAVE LASER FOCUS

When your life's purposes have a good sense of direction, your goals then have the power to provide you with the focus you need to know exactly how you should be spending your energy and time.

This energy is the input that is necessary to create any kind of output. When you have a goal, you can make a focal point where you can place your energy to be used to make a maximum reward.

GIVES US ACCOUNTABILITY

Goals make you accountable. Instead of just talking the talk, you are now obligated to walk the walk. This sense of accountability is essential with you, not anyone else. No one else knows the goals you create for yourself to accomplish. When you set specific targets, you are better able to stay the course.

CONCLUSION

Thank you and congratulations on making it to this part of the book. I hope you have learned a lot about different forms and techniques of behavioral therapy, and you are now better armed to reshape your life. By now, you should have a better understanding of the possible treatment program you want to try.

Which specific psychotherapy techniques have caught your attention? Are you into the goal-based CBT? Or perhaps you want to try practicing mindfulness exercise under ACT? You may choose to work alone and personalize your approach, but during the initial stages, it is ideal to work with a professional therapist who will serve as your partner in this journey towards living a life with meaning.

Continue your exploration of behavioral therapies, and try to do the following tips as part of the next steps:

Choose the top 3 specific techniques you want to try. Read more about them, and try to seek an appointment with professionals who are specializing in these techniques.

Join online forums, subscribe to blogs or seek membership with local clubs or organizations that will help you to immerse more with helpful techniques.

Reach out to people suffering from the same condition as you are and try to help them. The advantage of being empowered is that you can also share all the things you have gained - knowledge, skills, and attitude.

Please do not let this book be the end of your learning experience and the pursuit of self-empowerment. Keep in mind that the psychotherapy community is gearing for more research and in improving the treatment programs to help more people.

Your part is to look out for these developments so you can continue to grow and reshape your life and the lives of people you care about.